# From the Boiler Room to the Living Room

# From the Boiler Room to the Living Room

## WHAT THE COMING REVOLUTION IN THE FINANCIAL SERVICES INDUSTRY MEANS TO YOU AND YOUR CLIENTS

**Mitch Anthony**

**WILEY**

John Wiley & Sons, Inc.

Published by John Wiley & Sons, Inc., Hoboken, New Jersey.
Published simultaneously in Canada.

For general information on our other products and services or for technical support, please contact our Customer Care Department within the United States at (800) 762–2974, outside the United States at (317) 572–3993 or fax (317) 572–4002.

Wiley also publishes its books in a variety of electronic formats. Some content that appears in print may not be available in electronic books. For more information about Wiley products, visit our web site at www.wiley.com.

*Library of Congress Cataloging-in-Publication Data:*

Anthony, Mitch.
    From the boiler room to the living room: what the coming revolution in the financial services industry means to you and your clients / Mitch Anthony.
      p.  cm.
    Includes bibliographical references and index.
    ISBN 978–0–470–25509–4 (cloth)
      1. Financial planners.  2. Investment advisors.  3. Financial services industry.  I. Title.
    HG179.5.A577  2008
    332.1—dc22

          2008006158

Printed in the United States of America.
10  9  8  7  6  5  4  3  2  1

*This book is dedicated to Gil Weinreich,
editor par excellence for* Research *magazine whose
conscience is unfailing and whose pulse beats as
loudly and strongly as any man who has ever
loved this industry. He told me that I ought to
write from my heart to the heart of this industry.
What follows is the result of that invitation.*

# Contents

# Foreword

This is a book for aspirational financial advisors. It is for those who would earn their own living in the fertile fields of money and people and serve their clients from attitudes and altitudes of sacred trust and blessed stewardship. It is a book for those advisors whose hearts know that their client relationships are more than money. It is for those whose hearts' cores grasp that this work engages the harvests of life, work and soul.

These worthies should know when their work is done right and that this means that their work engages relationships that are grounded in the compassion and wisdom required to meet the demands of modern life, most especially its financial demands. It is for those who recognize that money and the vagaries of life are inextricably tied.

Money connects the circumstances of our lives. Money serves as our primary access to both survival basics and fulfilled personal destinies. It enables us to keep our promises to others. It drives how we show up in the world and relate to those around us for whatever reasons. Our relationships with money and finance are complex. They require a particular type of financial advisor who sees beyond the numbers.

If you are that type of financial advisor or would like to be, this book is a gift from Mitch Anthony to you. It is the real deal. There is nothing "soft" or "froufrou" about it. If you are that type of financial advisor, it gives voice to those thoughts and notions you know to be both fundamental and true. These pages are the essence of *thinking* and *acting* like a financial planner.

Anthony tells you why. Then he tells you how. He tells you how to combine your best thoughts with your best work to make a positive difference in people's lives. As a living bonus, he shows you how these best thoughts and best work also make for loyal clients and great business.

If, perchance, you are not that type of financial advisor, but would like to be, you might find inspiration here. Time and again, Anthony describes advisors who were soul sick from doing their work with the *boiler room* mentality. They did not know there was a different way. This book shows a different way. It puts real-life vitality into financial life planning processes.

It takes courage to work from one's soul. Throughout his book, Anthony shares himself. Unlike many authors purporting to tackle matters of soul, he makes it fearlessly real. Knowing all too well that financial life planning is more than intellectual indulgence or replicable formulae, Anthony shares his own life and some of his own significant encounters. Perhaps most importantly, he shares the emotional bounty of his own work with personal financial advisors. For those called to it, he views this work as holy and sacred.

This stands in stark contrast to the raw sales mentalities of the boiler room. As we read about practitioners of good heart providing financial advice "done right," the contrast with this way of thinking is very clear. It is curious. Why would anyone want to do business like that? Why would anyone want to do business with people who do business like that?

This is a book of wisdom and soul. It integrates art, craft, and wisdom with life, soul, and culture. It can serve as an operating manual for someone coming into the financial planning profession or as a source of personal inspiration for veteran financial advisors.

Be warned: This is not a "hard" book. It won't help you pass the test or up your testosterone count. You won't find charts, histories, or startling wealth enhancement strategies. As the title suggests, it is a book for living rooms, not ivory towers.

As with the uncommon virtue of common sense, it could be easy to take for granted the principles Anthony discusses. That would be a shame. With roots firmly planted in the financial services industries, the complexities of post–World War II money, and the urbanization of America, the role of financial advisor has emerged with difficulty over several decades. Grasping this book's significance requires perspectives steeped in history and an understanding of where we have been.

We must appreciate the postwar economic environment, the nature of money, and the pressures these have placed upon the lives and decisions of ordinary folks.

The economic environment continued to reflect postwar prosperity and chaos. The world was changing politically, demographically, and economically. Migrations from farms to cities changed the economic facts of life. People were dependent on financial assets as never before in history.

The financial planning profession's birth and "early childhood" in the 1970s came at a time of turmoil and financial chaos. The United States went off the gold standard. Not long after, we had the first oil crisis. Inflation ran at double digits; the stock market's volatility was shocking to investors. Not since the Great Depression had so many lost so much so fast. Inflation hit the housing markets and the baby boomers tore through everything, including real estate and the job markets. Financial fraud was rampant in the savings-and-loan world. This was also the case in that murky world known as the "penny stock" market. Tax rates were astronomical— as high as 90 percent on incremental income. It is little wonder that the term *tax shelter* entered common language for deals ranging from aggressive to outright deception.

Before World War II, there were not a lot of folks providing personal financial advice, either as advisors or salespeople. In the 1950s and 1960s, it was all sales. These were the halcyon days of Glass-Steagall. Not only were these men dedicated salespeople (and back then they were all men), they all represented a particular industry sector. There were insurance salespeople, stockbrokers, and bankers. They were separate. They got paid to sell, not serve. Moreover, for the most part, they could sell only one thing at a time—no mixing of insurance, securities, savings, tax advice, employee benefit planning, or retirement planning.

Meanwhile, many of these people learned grotesquely manipulative sales tricks. The worst of the lot worked in *churn 'n' burn* shops known as *boiler rooms*. For them, the term *penny stock* was a misnomer. It was often worth less.

It is unfair to suggest that all financial advisors worked in the venal pits known as "boiler rooms." However, we can accurately observe that the financial services industry was not client-centric. The best of this lot sold high-commission cash-value life insurance or high-commission securities. For all of them, the name of the game was *production*. Production meant sales—and only sales. It did not mean you had added to someone's long-term security or helped them with wealth building or otherwise addressed their relationships with money or the money forces. *Goals? Meaning? Happiness?* Perish the thought. At the end of the day, if you did not move product, you simply were *not* a "producer."

In the late 1960s, some farsighted folks thought this was nuts. They saw that individuals needed to coordinate their finances and get their advice from a single source. They thought that people deserved to get good financial product that would perform as described and promised when they put their money down. They used terms like *due diligence* and *best interests of the client*. They declared that there was a better way to work with individuals and their complex relationships with the money forces.

They were aspirational. Starting with just a handful of good souls, then growing into hundreds, then thousands, they founded professional associations and started an academic institution. They established standards of practice and codes of ethics. Spreading internationally by sheer force of will, common sense, and pure idealism, these individuals took on five of the strongest industries on the planet: insurance, securities, banking, law, and accounting. They broke from the restraints of law and custom to do their work in harmony with their souls and meet the needs of people desperate for comprehensive help.

Not that the rest of the financial services industry was much help. As cross-selling came of age and the term *financial planning* entered our vocabularies, these folks did not see improved client services. They saw "enhanced product delivery systems." Psychology was about customer manipulation. Psychology served sales, not souls.

Financial advisors continued to ignore the interior. In its adolescence, financial planning was still mostly about sales or technical proficiency. Many made fun of the "touchy-feely" stuff. They called it "soft." It was perceived as the functional equivalent of women's work. Real men did the numbers. Meanwhile, the financial services industry missed few opportunities to tell aspiring financial planners that we were all "just salesmen" after all.

It was lonely for those visionaries who could see the connections between money and life. There were few exercises to help financial advisors get to know their clients better. Even those few pioneers who saw the relationships between money and soul lacked a viable vocabulary for their work. We did not have the words to describe replicable situations or practices. Now we can see. What we can see, we can name. We need the words this book provides.

It is hard to remember that the skills that seem so natural and right were virtually unknown not so very long ago. Yet, for perspective, we must remember that we have grown this garden from seed.

We did not have the words. We did not have the exercises. We did not have the perspective. Though it can be thoughtfully argued that the best books on personal finance had been written 2,000 years ago, our resources were sparse nonetheless. Now we have books like this one.

Mitch Anthony gets it. He understands that our relationships with money are sacred. He realizes that our relationships with money are crucial to our qualities of life and the promises we have made. He comprehends that financial advisors are not just worthy of respect, but that they, in fact, occupy vital, critical positions of sacred trust in the lives of their clients. He knows that financial advice done right is critical to lives well lived and worth living. "Done right" means bringing a mixture of right brain, left brain, and a good heart. "Done right" means, wisdom, craft and understanding.

*From the Boiler Room to the Living Room* is a guide to doing this work right. It is a compendium of best practices. It enhances and expands financial planning's garden of knowledge. It cultivates this garden's bounty and makes it accessible. It makes the world a better place.

*Richard B. Wagner, JD, CFP*
*Editor of* InsideMoney.org

# Acknowledgments

I would like to acknowledge Debbie, my wife, for her ever-present faith and editorial TLC; agent Cynthia Zigmund for her keen eye and high standards; and researchers Megan Stubbendeck and Molly Jo Nyman for their devoted passion and curiosity. To the many leaders in the industry—too many to name here—who "get it" and are doing their absolute best to help this industry evolve—you know who you are—I thank you for your encouragement in taking on a systemic dragon. To the many advisors who have approached me over the years and told me their stories of how they have changed their lives and businesses by taking a life-centered, relationship-centered approach, I wish to acknowledge your courage in leading the way.

# Preface

*You have to stop in order to change direction.*

—Erich Fromm

*The foundation of the new world must be laid by those who have the courage to change the old; by those whose arteries are still soft and clear, whose minds are still active and whose hearts are still generous.*

—Earl Warren

For the past decade I have been a front-line eyewitness to the birth pangs of an industry being reborn. In shaking off its old skin and presenting itself anew, the industry has been wrestling with what it was, what it is, and what it must become to remain relevant in the culture it serves.

*Metamorphosis* is a very good word for what has been happening. The old, original model crawled—for the last decade it has been in various stages of cocooning and is just now beginning to emerge as a species capable of greater accomplishment.

The original model for this industry was cast from the boilerplate of the boiler room. The blueprint was designed by manufacturers and vendors who wanted to distribute *product* through various *producers;* their first and foremost consideration was constantly increasing *production.*

In a sales culture, the emphasis is—for better or worse—on the provider's bottom line, not the clients. *What have you done for me lately; Smiling and dialing; Turn that conversation into a sale;* and *Get your numbers up* are all motivational mantras from the boiler room archetype.

But a funny thing happened on the way to the top-producers club.

Products and processes were commoditized at an accelerated rate due to the proliferation of information on the Internet. Prices began to fall, never to recover, and product brokering value propositions were left flapping in the wind.

With an early recognition of the evolution from salesperson to professional advisor, many apt and conscientious providers began to identify the need for a better and more holistic process and, in their search, found their way to certified financial planner (CFP), certified insurance counselor (CIC), as well as various other courses of learning and distinction in order to raise their knowledge, increase their competency, and elevate their standing in society.

Industry scrutiny came with all the subtlety of a searchlight at midnight (some would say it was overdue and some would say it was overdone—perhaps both are right) and left an industry saddled with a labyrinth of paperwork, restrictions, and paranoia.

What began as a company-centric sales industry is now evolving, rather quickly, into a client-centric service industry. Products are still involved but they are no longer the primary point of conversation. Product pushers are flailing futilely at this change-up pitch, swinging far too early in the conversation, only to look foolish for doing so. The products now must complement the service, which is based largely on intellectual capital and relational competence, not on the product of the week. The "smilin' and dialin'," aficionados are becoming dinosaurs, and nobody wants to follow in their tracks.

The money conversation began to change as well. People who were once simply expected to call clients with "investment ideas" were now expected to share solutions and strategies and engage in number-crunching processes. Then, out of the blue, they were suddenly expected to have "life-centered" conversations and to discover who their clients were and what mattered most to them. Who had time for this?

Many senior executives in this industry have articulated to me their recognition of this evolution and their frustration with trying to "teach old dogs new tricks" and in trying to figure out what type of person they should be recruiting for the future—the future being not yet clearly defined.

These are the birth pangs of an industry being reborn and recast—*from the boiler room to the living room.* The cocoon has already begun breaking. We are seeing glimpses of what will come forth. It will be a greater creature than what previously existed, but not without a struggle.

The difference between evolution (what naturally evolves over time) and revolution (what is forced to happen in a shorter time) lies largely with "volition"—that is, the will of the people to make it so.

The democratic system that our country enjoys was inevitable. Such was the opinion of our founding fathers who decided to force the issue. Why should men not be free to do with their lives as they wish without interference from the privileged few? This thought inspired a band of republicans to demand better and to settle for nothing less.

There is a strain of democratization at work in the current revolution that I see taking shape in financial services. People have a right to know exactly what is happening with their money, who is profiting from it, who is telling the truth, and who is playing games with their livelihood. They will no longer settle for being "sold" or manipulated for someone else's gain.

If we were to draft a client bill of rights, it might help our policies meet the test of conscience and might include the following:

- A client has a right to advice that is advisory in nature and not a euphemism for the "product of the month."
- A client has a right to a competent and concerned professional who respects the sacred nature of their hard-fought earnings.
- A client has a right to transparency around all fees and costs, up-front and back-end included.
- A client has a right to be understood as a person and not just as a number.
- A client has a right to trust that the custodian of their wealth will preserve and conscientiously protect that wealth for the sake of survival and living well.

There is work to do.

At a recent industry think tank with leaders present from a number of leading firms (manufacturers and retailers), I asked our discussion group how many could say that there was true alignment between the firm's interests down to the individual advisor's interest and extending to the best interest of the client.

The silence in the room was eerie.

Finally, a respected industry veteran said, "This silence is a sad statement." And another chimed in, "I guess we've got some work to do."

## Looking on the Inside

Any person who has worked in the arena of personal financial planning for long knows that money is a complex topic. The complexity I am referring to, however, refers not to the allocation, placement, manipulation, or management and distribution of the assets, which indeed, are complex enough. These complexities are concerned with what could be called the *external* realities regarding money. External realities are what the financial services business is all about: How much do you have? Where is it? How could we do better? How much will you need? What are your goals?

It is this last question that has become a staple of discovery in the industry that has caused practitioners to cross unwittingly from the external to the *internal* aspects of finance. Soon, clients are revealing people and places and events that are important in their lives. Quite often, they begin talking, with a palpable amount of emotion, of how they would like to see their story evolve. It doesn't take a clergyperson, psychoanalyst, or a philosopher to perceive that the topic of money, merely material and quantitative on the surface, has multiple layers of trust or distrust, emotion, history, meaning, feeling, and intention below that surface.

You are now in the realm of *internal finance.*

Very little has been written on the internal side of money. In the next decade we will begin to see a proliferation from this emerging field of study and observation, works that will explore the soulish side of money.

What does this money mean?

What price was paid to obtain it?

Whose lives will be impacted and how?

What are your greatest hopes and fears related to this money?

How do you view money, and how are you most comfortable dealing with it?

## The Soulful Financial Advisor

If you view yourself simply as a tactician or money mechanic, you may say to yourself, "I have no interest in such questions," but I contend that, as a practitioner, you cannot avoid them for long. Someone in your organization needs to build meaningful relationships with clients in order to create a stable business. A meaningful relationship is just that—a relationship *full of meaning*. It would then follow that a meaningful relationship around money *extends to understanding what this money means to someone's life and future.*

You are now squarely situated in the *discussion* of *internal finance*. Another way to frame the discussion is that, after mastering the left-brain side of money management, we are now being challenged to master the right-brain side of the business.

Until recently, the financial services industry was not ready to hear a message that delved into the emotional, meaningful, and soulful implications of the financial advisory business. But the confluence of 9/11, a sobering bear market and revelations of corruptive conflicts of interest has provided the perfect storm that has turned the industry's focus back to building meaningful and lasting relationships with clients.

This is a time for turning things inside out, for examining the innermost soul of an industry that has held the hopes and dreams of hundreds of millions of people in its stewardship and has often failed in that stewardship.

I believe the financial services industry is being turned inside out for good reason. Too many games have been played with assets that represent people's lives, hopes and dreams, and quality of life. We all understand that money is a serious topic, but too often the institutions that claim to know the seriousness of the topic have demonstrated otherwise in flippant, foolish, and even felonious fashion.

When trusted institutions and fraternal organizations are found to be exploiting their members and clients and self-serving at the trough of their clients' travails the time has come for deep industry-wide soul searching. If, as Aristotle said, the unexamined life is worthless, how much more worthless is the unexamined industry. This industry has been duly examined from the exterior by the courts and the fourth estate, and now the time for internal examination arrives where a new and genuine to-the-core type of industry and professional can emerge and be recognized.

I believe the audience is ready. There is a philosophical hunger in the industry among mature practitioners and firms desiring to demonstrate new standards of integrity to build individual advisor-client relationships that will transcend market jitters, trying economic climates, and industry foibles.

Scores of firms are adapting to the themes and models I introduced for building client relationships in *Storyselling for Financial Advisors, The New Retirementality,* and *Your Clients for Life.* This book is the most soul-searching yet in terms of coming to grips with what it is going to take to restore and rebuild trust within each individual practice and for the industry at large.

*From the Boiler Room to the Living Room* explores the following issues:

- Where the industry has failed itself and its clients in the past and how to restore trust.
- Large-scale adjustments the industry must consider to meet the evolving needs ands demands of clients.
- How to gain a greater understanding of what money represents to your client's life and well-being.
- How to develop dialogues that will build long-term trusting relationships.

My best intention for this book is that it will act as an introduction to the broad and deep territories and avenues of internal finance. I hope that through this series of discussions we can come to a place of comfort and understanding that what we see on the surface with money is just the beginning of the story, and that those with a *seeing eye* would raise their dialogues and relationships to a place of the highest integrity and empathy.

There are decisions that firms and individuals in this industry still need to make. At the end of each chapter I will offer a *ReSOULution*—a decision based on internal insight—that I sense is necessary to carry this revolution and industry transformation forward. Ultimately, it is left to each individual to accept nothing less than the best in order for the whole to be transformed.

The financial services ranks are filled with great thinkers and generous hearts that have seen the writing on the wall for some time. They have been doing their best to reshape, reform, and reframe their firms, their offerings, and their advisors' value propositions.

Many of these revolutionaries are fighting extreme uphill battles within their organizational cultures, which cannot perceive how to exist outside of the boiler room template. I have seen a few of these good men and women tire and leave the battle but know of many more who have dug in their heels and are determined to lead their firms in and through this metamorphosis period. Once the industry sheds this cocoon and realizes what it can be, we will all benefit: client, advisor, and firm alike.

# PART I

# INDUSTRY RESOULUTIONS

Most of us are by now aware of what has been wrong in the financial services industry. Somewhere along the way the industry lost its way or, in some cases, never set out on the right path to start with, and has reached a dead end. This part is not about pointing fingers and pointing out the obvious, but rather about first examining *why* the industry's value proposition and ultimate reputation ended up where it did; and, second, about offering a more lasting, more integral, and more perpetual value proposition that will benefit both client and industry, in that order.

# CHAPTER 1

# If These Walls Could Talk

*The most certain science is conscience.*

—Viktor Frankl

Anthropologists studying peoples deep within the Amazon came across a tribe that had an unusually high mortality rate and short life expectancy. They studied the eating, drinking, medicinal, and health habits of the tribe and could find nothing to explain the phenomenon. Eventually, they found the problem in the very walls of the houses these people lived in.

The tribe built their homes from river mud, which contained a species of bug that carried a virus. By using this mud for the walls of their home, they were literally building houses of death. Upon discovering this, the anthropologists sat down with the elders of the tribe to reveal their findings. The elders dismissed the anthropologists so they could decide on the issue. They later told the anthropologists they had decided to do nothing—it would be too difficult to find a new way of building shelter. It was the only way the tribe knew.

This same story could be told about some investment firms as well: the dying stock/fund jockey and the diseased investment house that is infected in its very walls with a virus known as self-centeredness. This virus causes its landlords to believe that the client who enters the house exists only to meet the needs of the house and to serve its own interests. Some of the leaders in these houses are perplexed by the number of investment advisors falling by the wayside and the decline of worthwhile clients coming to visit. In declining markets many of these landlords blame the wayward attitude of the market rather than their own attitude and actions for this demise.

How do these same leaders explain away the fact that thousands of client-centered financial planning practices grow and maintain during the same market periods? Those financial professionals whose houses are built with the lasting materials of servitude and self-transcendence are flourishing as never before. The problem, as illustrated above with the Amazonian tribe, exists within the very walls of the infected investment firm office: Those who live within these walls breathe toxic air each and every day and, as a result, mortality rates are high.

The leader of the infected investment firm, whose team suffers the greatest mortality, most likely caught this virus through direct or secondary exposure to Ayn Rand's philosophy of objectivism that seduces executives and managers into thinking that the greater good is ultimately met by pursuing one's own self-interests. As the industry headlines of the last few years have demonstrated, this philosophy has been practiced in corporate corner offices to the point of their undoing. If Atlas is shrugging off anything these days, it is this blind and foolish philosophy that purports to help others while only helping oneself. Put another way, it would be like the pig saying his only motive for slurping at the trough is because he knows he will one day be man's breakfast. The pig overeats jealously only because it is his nature to behave in a hoggish fashion.

The breadth and permeation of this virus has been brought to the public consciousness from the business page to the front page and—as a grave indicator of its endemic state—to the comics page, with *Dilbert* strips satirizing the selfish advisor. Online brokerage houses joined in the satire with the "Let's put some lipstick on this pig" ads showing advisors acting like boiler room operators, and posterized human images lamenting how their brokers were ripping them off. These images and messages contributed as well to the heightened awareness by exploiting the techniques of exploitation. Some recent experiences have driven the point home even more.

A friend who is an executive for a mutual fund company called to tell me that his father, whose retirement assets have shrunk considerably, can no longer sleep by night nor relax by day. He joined his father on a trip to talk to his advisor. The first thing my friend noted about his father's advisor was that he was unaware that his client had been retired for the last year and a half! Within 10 minutes he was trying to sell a new product to my friend's father. My friend told me he had to muster all his restraint to keep from reaching across the desk and choking this advisor. He told me, "I'm in this business and I understand the need to sell products but, my God, this guy had no interest in my father's life or dilemma whatsoever.

*Why doesn't this "advisor" know more or care more about his clients? Because the walls of the house are infected, and, as a result, so is he.*

My accountant e-mailed to tell me that a client of his had come to see him because she had stopped receiving checks from her annuity and had visited her advisor and was confused about his "advice." He had advised her to sell the annuity and buy into some bonds that would mature in 15 years. She wondered if that was a good idea given that she was 81 years old at present. The accountant told her he would look into it further. Upon review, he found that the recommended bond fund was almost identical to what she was allocated to within the annuity. The only advantage going was to the advisor, who would profit from the transaction.

*Why would an advisor offer exploitative self-interest as advice? Because the walls of the house are infected, and, as a result, so is he.*

Several years ago an advisor had recommended that I purchase sizeable stakes in two telecom stocks just before they began their precipitous fall. I wasn't blaming the advisor for the recommendations (after all, I had agreed with his idea at the time), but I was bothered by the fact that I had not heard from him in almost a year as these investments plummeted to 10 percent of their original value. Not a single phone call. I decided to make the call to him. When he answered, he said, "Oh, I'm so glad you called. My company doesn't allow us to call accounts anymore that have fallen below $____ in value." I remarked on the irony of the fact that it was his company's recommendations that caused my account to fall into their "not important" category. I transferred my account the next day.

*Why would an advisor not care? Because the walls of the house are infected, and, as a result, so is he.*

## A New Campaign

An advisor working for a bank came up to me after a speech with his eyes filling up and said, "I had decided before this meeting that I just couldn't do this anymore. If you can show me a way to center what I do around the life and needs of my client, I will have hope. I have turned down the volume on my conscience for the last time."

One can breathe toxic air only so long. At some point, self-preservation kicks in.

You may have noticed that there has been a concerted effort of late to change the image of the house by advertising to reflect themes of client-centeredness and client concern.

As with all paradigm shifts, there are some genuine parties and efforts at work and there are pretenders. The genuine parties are focused on bringing assimilation between their ads and their advisors. The disingenuous and half-hearted simply spend money on the ads.

Do some of these houses believe that the problem is only with the sign on the house? Does it escape their notice that the problem is with the air one must breathe once we're inside? How long will it take before the perceptions of the advertisements become the reality of the client? Is there a process in place to bridge the promise of the advertisement with the practice of the advisor? Is there any line or strategic process that connects the two? The advertisements may be different, but until the theme of the Monday morning "sales meeting" is different, the death toll will continue to rise.

Until company culture issues are addressed, the inveterate mistakes that have made headlines will prove incurable. Nothing gives away the careless conscience like talking out of two sides of one's mouth: telling advisors to do their best to serve their clients, but also making sure you do your best with them pushing XYZ fund this week. If the mistakes of the last decade have not brought the issue of self-centeredness to the surface, what will it take? Exploitation continues as long as the virus is allowed to grow.

The selling of financial advice can be a noble trade. But it cannot be noble if it is simply a masquerade for a financial carnival act. There is a better way.

Good advisors can and do play heroic roles in the lives of their clients. Let's assume that every product designed intends to solve a problem or meet a need. The product is good if the intention of the product is good and the price affixed is competitive. This product is designed to meet a real need, so where does the danger lie in bringing this solution to the public? There is really only one variable that opens the door to danger and keeps the selling of advice from being respectful and dignified. Every professional also knows appropriateness can be solved only through thorough and sincere discovery.

One size does not fit all. But pressure is applied by the landlords of the house to "move" that product, and as long as the message of moving products supersedes the message, this industry will be replete with advisors trying to cram size 11 feet into size 9 shoes.

Not too long ago, I witnessed a sales training session within the industry. The trainer commenced his training paradigm with this premise, "First, create a need." I was dumbfounded. Create a need presupposes that there are no legitimate needs in the life of this client—therefore the advisor must manipulate his perceptions to act as a springboard for his sales presentation. I challenge any advisor to find any client conversation where, with enough effort to understand the client's situation and goals, a real need would not appear that could be addressed with a product or process you now offer. It is a self-absorbed and lazy approach to think we must "create the need."

## The Soul of the Matter

Appropriateness is ultimately a question of conscience and soul: Am I trying to create the perception that this is needed to meet my own agenda, or am I trying to find the client's real needs by offering the most appropriate fix for those needs? The first sign of recovery from this virus is that the advisor begins to take a much keener interest in the lives of his clients and becomes much more intrigued in the discovery part of the conversation than in product pushing. A strange paradox begins playing out in the practices of those recovering from the virus: *the less time they spend pushing products and the more time they spend discovering the lives and hopes of their clients, the more products and services they end up distributing. But now all product sales are highly appropriate.* Doing the right thing pays off.

Though many campaigns reflect a sincere desire to form better relationships, until the house is rebuilt with a different material, the core of the virus will not go away. It is not a media campaign that is needed but a conversion of the very soul of the business. Self-interest must give way to what philosopher Viktor Frankl called "self-transcendence," more commonly known as "seeing past your own nose." The industry can no longer afford shortsightedness, opportunism, or superficial relationships.

When advisors come to work and are greeted with a Monday morning pep talk about building better relationships, when the motivation is about focusing on the long run and the big picture, when the focus is about discovering what's going on in clients' lives and about providing services that match the needs arising in those conversations, then and only then will behavior begin to change.

As is always the case, some chiefs will be slow to embrace this transformation because they have built their houses with mud from the river and don't know any other way to build them (and their paychecks hinge on the behavior that results from this virus). They will continue to move market share to those tribes whose chiefs have already recognized the source of the trouble and are rebuilding their houses and to those tribes who never used mud from the river in the first place.

"So some advisors don't last long," these resistant chiefs will muse, "so some advisors are burnt out and some clients are going elsewhere. There will always be casualties. We just need to push harder on the tribe that remains. Our business is about meeting our bottom line." As is the case with many untreated diseases, eventually it will kill these houses and the advisors within.

*And so we see that the virus of self-interest has the potential to infect every last brain cell.*

## Working in Infected Walls

I once consulted two days a week for a company that had serious mold problems in their walls. Being sensitive to molds because of asthma and allergies, I would begin wheezing and struggling for breath within an hour of arriving and constantly fought for breath the days I worked there. I noticed that others in the company were struggling as well, so I went to the CEO and told him the problem. He looked at me like I was a weakling and dismissed the complaint with a huff. He simply was not willing to acknowledge the negative impact of the toxic air in his office. His attitude was that a real man or woman could take it. Tired of getting sick at his office, I canceled my consulting contract and was amazed at how great it felt to be able to breathe clean air again.

In this discussion we must not overlook the damage this virus has done in the lives of the advisor forced to breathe the air within the walls of an infected house. Too many advisors are not feeling well these days because of pressure to produce on one side and numbness to clients on the other. How long can a good man or woman breathe this air without collapsing?

A few months ago, an advisor who told me he worked within infected walls came to a session where we were discussing how to conduct better dialogues with clients. He was full of enthusiasm as we practiced meaningful and productive conversations that had no manipulative undertones. I stopped the training and told him, "I don't think you realize that this day is going to make things worse for you, not better. You are charged up about having a real, life-centered financial dialogue, and when you go back another sort of conversation is going to be forced upon you so that you can force it upon your clients. When that happens. you will be more miserable than you are now because now you know how to take the client dialogue to a different level."

It is better to have never known the truth than to know and not be able to practice it.

Within a week I received a phone call from this advisor. He told me he had gone home and had some of the most meaningful and trust-building conversations he had ever had with his clients. Within two days, his "chief" was deriding him for not moving more of product X. This advisor informed me that, as predicted, his latter state was worse that the first. He just couldn't force himself to have that other sort of conversation anymore, and the daily pressure to do so was making him miserable.

He knew that he now had two choices: (1) have a heart-to-heart with his firm to see if they will allow him to operate in the fashion he needed to, or (2) move to an environment that matches his values completely.

## Your Client's Bottom Line

What better example can we find of the diseased walls on Wall Street than the auction-rate security debacle? To the consumer, this sloppily researched and imprudently designed instrument was sold as a "cash-equivalent." What does that term mean to you? It sounds a lot like something that operates the same as money, liquid and with no risk of loss of principal, doesn't it? Of course it does. Try explaining this to clients who can't get their "cash equivalents" back.

There are stricken investors attempting to retrieve their monies who are being impeded, most notably by closed-end fund managers, some of whom gambled heavily in auction-rate notes.

Some experts have suggested that managers could, if they chose to, sell underlying securities and use the proceeds to buy back common shares. This would reduce the size of the funds and allow them to redeem some of the preferred shares they had issued to increase the fund's yield. This would at least calm shareholders' fears and repair the damage of a deceptively labeled investment. But such a remedy would result in reducing assets in the funds as well as managers' fees, which are based on the amount of assets managed.

Imagine a scenario where an investment firm takes unnecessary risks, falsifies the nature of those risks to the consumer, and, under the heat of scrutiny, is more interested in protecting their own stakes than those of the clients they supposedly serve?

This is not hard to imagine within infected walls.

The quickest and surest cure for the virus is to adopt the client's bottom line as your own. The client's bottom line is about their needs, comfort levels, hopes, and concerns. Where your products and services cross orbits with the client's bottom line is the point at which all prosperity occurs—materially, relationally, and internally.

For the company with infected walls, the quantitative bottom line will not improve until this qualitative bottom is established and pursued with vigor and sincerity.

When the bottom line becomes placing a higher importance on the client's goals than those of the individual advisor or the investment house, we will know that self-transcendence is being practiced. When the conversation is about uncovering real needs and applying tailored solutions, we will know the house has been rebuilt with materials that are safe both for the advisor *and* his clients.

This house will stand against any storm the markets can bring because human nature in adverse circumstances is to seek refuge—places and people in whose presence they feel safe. For the truly client-centered practice, storms are a time of expansion and reaching out to the wounded and confused, not a time of shrinkage. If this has not been the case for your house, it might be time to inspect the walls.

### ReSOULution

Check the toxicity level in the house within which you dwell. Are the walls infected? Is the culture sincere or sincerely misguided? Is duplicity present between the image and the behavior toward clients? Consider the impact of a toxic environment on your own well-being. Breathe toxic air long enough and you will feel your energy waning, your thoughts lacking sharpness and clarity, and maybe even the slow dissipation of your will and resolve to do better.

*Your clients are tenants in your house. You and they both deserve to breathe purified air.*

# CHAPTER 2

# Speedometers and Odometers

*The pocketbook opens up no wider than the mind's breadth of understanding.*

—Mitch Anthony

hief executive squirrel, Theo Skouros, called an emergency meeting in the Executive Hollow. It was time for our spring season review of financial results, which had come to be known as the "Easter Hangover" by the troops.

"These numbers aren't where they need to be. If we don't hit our target, Walnut Street will have us for lunch. Flying Squirrel, Inc. doesn't miss its numbers!"

By hook or by crook, FSI had managed for the past 15 years to show season-over-season improvement in earnings—no small miracle when you consider the fact that acorns fall only in the fall season. This had been accomplished with a stealthy combination of labor and legerdemain.

"Mr. Skouros, we just barely made the winter number," offered chief financial squirrel, Cornelius Grey, "but managed to pack enough away to use in the summer to hit the number we'll need then. We could move early and sell that inventory in order to get the spring number we need."

We all knew it was a softball tossed up from Grey to Skouros. Grey was no fool but, on occasion, made himself as such to service the ego of our

*(Continued)*

CEO and founder. Grey had no need to be a hero, but he did have a need for a regular paycheck, and with his gift for numbers and willingness to be abused, he certainly had a found a track for collecting.

"And then get our tails whacked off in the summer! Get real, Grey," Skouros blasted back. "We need to get creative around here. Somebody bring an idea that won't kill us three months down the road."

Senior vice squirrel of sales, Dutch Van Elm, stood up. "Boss, I've had this idea for a while and think this might be the time. As you know, every fall we end up with about a 20 percent "throwaway rate" on bad nuts that are sitting out back by the marsh. Nobody's going to want to eat them, but why couldn't we sell them to Beaver Industries, who've been talking about growing their own trees for some time?"

"Have you lost your mind, Dutch?" Grey objected. "Those acorns are no good. They won't grow, and anybody who looks at them will know they are rotten—you can see the holes in them!"

"I don't want to hear what *won't* work here," Skouros stared down Grey. "I want to know what *will* work."

"Boss, I got it all worked out," Van Elm offered, slapping his tail furiously against the floor. "First of all, all these acorns need is a little 'cosmetic' treatment. Second, I'll grant Grey the fact that some of them might not grow, but it's marginal and by the time Beaver, Inc. figures that out we're two years down the road and we simply answer by saying it was due to their inexperience with husbandry or the climate.

"*Some* of them won't grow?!? Cosmetic treatment?!? Van Elm, just when I think I've heard it all, somebody from sales comes up with this," Grey sneered. "We certainly wouldn't be raising any eyebrows by buying huge inventories of varnish now, would we?"

"What sort of 'cosmetic treatment' are you proposing?" asked Skouros. "We sure as oak don't need a varnish scandal."

"I've got a solution all worked out and have already tested it with the lab. It will take a little work, but it's simple. You stew the acorns in a sap/water mix. The bonding element in the sap causes the brown color to adhere to the discolored 'wounds' in the product. It truly has a healing effect," Van Elm explained, all smiles now.

"I suppose you would consider paint a 'healing' remedy for rotten wood as well, huh, Van Elm?" Grey hollered, throwing his claws out for effect.

"Enough of the sarcasm, Grey. We certainly can't solve problems with sarcasm," Skouros said in his most soothing tone, doing a sort of goofy Gandhi impression, bringing calm to the irrationality ruling the dray at the moment.

Skouros dignified the insanity by probing further, in a tone of sincere diligence.

"Van Elm, what kind of return do you think we can get on this initiative at going rates?"

"That's where this deal really shines." Dutch gleamed, "I go to Beaver Industries and tell them we need to meet our winter number, and that to do it we're willing to sell inventory at a deep discount. If anybody understands that, it's those guys, after the beating they took two seasons ago on their waterworks contract. They need to diversify, and we're helping them into the lumber biz at a discount. We sell this inventory at 50 percent off the normal rate and we still book almost a million."

"Grey, where does that put us regarding spring expectations?" Skouros was performing a stare-down toward Grey now.

Grey was grinding his teeth, unable to look back at Skouros.

"Grey! Where does that put us?" Skouros repeated in a forcibly calmed tone.

Grey could barely spit out the words, "Just above what the street is calling for the spring report. But Theo, a year or two from now this thing could come back to bite us big time."

"A year or two from now, if we don't hit our numbers," Skouros answered, "this tree will be cut down and probably sold for lumber to Beaver, Inc. We don't have the luxury of harvesting nuts four seasons a year, so we need to use our ingenuity around here. And speaking of ingenuity, we need to start thinking now about the summer numbers and what we'll need to do to hit that target. Meeting adjourned."

*From Mitch Anthony, "Squirreling Away the Future"*

An advisor who works for a Fortune 500 company walked up to me after I had delivered a talk to his firm on building client relationships. He offered the following excerpt from his firm's Monday morning "fire up the troops" meeting:

"'Do the right thing for your clients, take good care of them,' we are told at the beginning of the meeting," he shared. "And the meeting gets closed with, 'and all of you need to sell more of this XYZ product. Let's go get 'em.'" He continued, "One can't help but be a bit dismayed at the hypocrisy of thinking you are serving people by pushing product."

"If you can," I encouraged him, "try to look past your bosses' mixed messages to the machinery that drives such a message. When you trace it all the way back, you will find the Wizard of Oz controlling everything from behind a curtain. The Wizard is looking at the upcoming Wall Street expectations, meaning the problem is the quarterly report. It's a strange sort of fiscal insanity that you won't find very often outside of publicly held firms."

## Running the Race

Think of it this way: Quarterly reporting is like running a four-leg relay race where each quarter mile must time out just a little better than the previous quarter. So, instead of running the race with your absolute best effort, you must conjure a pace and effort to demonstrate the result the crowd is expecting. It inevitably will lead to manipulated performances, insincere demonstrations of effort, and, as recent history has illustrated in marquee fashion, manipulated reporting.

This absurdity ignores the normal, natural course of growth (with lines that show peaks, valleys, spurts, and flattening periods) and substitutes them with artificial lines that display a never-ending staircase upward and onward. Achieving such an unnatural course of growth not only takes imagination, it also places the players (from the top down) in a constant pressure cooker. Earnings expectations, like water, run downhill. Everything and everyone in its path is affected because the water just keeps coming. There is no time to think or to breathe.

As someone who works with companies across the industry, I cannot help but notice the difference between the quarterly reporting culture and the private company culture. Both parties seem to be motivated to succeed, but the blood pressure seems to run much higher in the former. Take away the tension of unrealistic growth patterns and people are allowed to find a pace and pattern for growth that is livable—and ultimately more successful—over the long run.

## Wave of the Future?

A vanguard of publicly traded firms has now banded together to try to orient investors toward the long-term view. One of the companies, Google, sent a letter to investors in which founders Larry Page and Sergey Brin stated that they were pursuing high-risk, high-reward ideas despite short-term earnings pressures and asked their investors to use fortitude and take a long-term view.

According to an article in the *Harvard Business Review* featuring Judith Samuelson, this vanguard is composed of 20 companies with a large enough cumulative market capitalization to persuade the market at large. Participants in this "let's think about and orient toward the long-term" effort include IBM, General Electric, and PepsiCo. They are meeting to investigate *principles* and to design practices that promote long-term competitiveness over short-term shortsightedness. That's the good news.

On the other side of the ledger we learn from a recent study that only 59 percent of executives would pursue a *positive* net present value project if it meant missing the quarterly earnings consensus, and—it gets worse—78 percent say they would sacrifice value, in some cases major value, in order to smooth earnings.

This coming from the guys who are telling everyone at company meetings to "do what's right for our clients." But you can't really blame the chief, can you, when all the chief is doing is following the system that everyone relies on? And what a lovely system it has proven to be. The Conference Board's Blue Ribbon Commission on restoring public trust blamed "short-termism" for contributing to business malfeasance.

Duh.

I am not foolish or megalomaniacal enough to believe that my humble pen is going to convince any firm to rethink its publicly listed shortsightedness, but I will unflinchingly challenge each and every one of them to rethink its message to their retail representatives. And I would provoke this rethinking process with a word of encouragement: the growth you see from investing in long-term relationships with your clients will, in the long term, lead to far superior financial results because (1) clients will sense the dearth of self-serving undercurrents and be inclined to entrust more assets; and (2) good, principled advisors will flourish in and be loyal to such an environment.

## Measuring Success with What?

A client from a large multinational firm called me about coming to train his advisors on how to build long-term, lifetime relationships with their clients. This firm had been running a sales turnstile for quite some time and could see the writing on the wall.

I told this gentleman that I would be more than happy to come and train accordingly, but on a conditional basis—that they integrate the long-term relational value into their compensation plans. I told him, "If you're not going to pay for a desired behavior, my training on the new behavior is a waste of time for both of us."

He agreed with this point and told me that a proposed change in the pay plan would accomplish exactly this and that we would postpone the training until the pay plan went into effect. I can barely express to you how refreshing it was to hear someone in a position of leadership admit to the silliness of trying to say one thing and pay for another.

An obsession with short-term measures for the sake of meeting short-term goals does not help and, in fact, clearly sabotages the goal of reaching a permanent destination of trusted advisor relationships.

If you want to insure success in the long term, you need to use an instrument for measuring success that is gauged for the long term and employ the use of that instrument consistently. If, in fact, the right thing to do to is to invest ourselves in the long-term well-being of our clients, then the numbers should and will affirm that verity.

Firms need to decide how they want to proceed, based on the reasons discussed in this chapter. Think of it this way: you are going to run your firm either by the speedometer (miles per hour) or the odometer (miles made in the journey), but you can't have it both ways. Common sense invokes us all to work for the long-term relationship, but common sense isn't going to show up in the relationship if it doesn't first show up in the advisor's paycheck. People inevitably behave in the way they are paid to behave. The mixed message on Monday morning doesn't get mixed in the head of the retail provider. By and large, they will do what they get paid to do.

Selling by the speedometer resembles the carnival industry more than it resembles the advice industry. When you are told to squeeze as much revenue as possible out of every interaction (mph), how do you keep "carny"-style manipulation and marksmanship out of your approach. It is a poisoned sort of thinking, and it reviles honest advisors, who find themselves thinking such thoughts against their better selves. I have heard confessions of such from conscientious types, replete with descriptions of self-loathing for having had such thoughts. These are good people I'm talking about, who have felt they were being asked to act against the best version of themselves, only because the Wizard demands it from behind his curtain.

Imagine having this conversation: "Mr. and Mrs. Jones, our firm is built on the principle of getting to know who our clients are and building relationships that serve you over a lifetime. Now, if you don't mind, our hour is almost up and you haven't decided on any insurance or investments yet. Which product sounds better for you today?"

No one in their right mind would proffer something so silly, yet organizational structures and measures for success are built on this very approach.

Have we completely lost touch with sanity in our business models? Being a resident of Rochester, Minnesota, which is home to the world-renowned Mayo Clinic, I decided to put this question to a psychiatrist.

"How would you describe this condition of focusing/obsessing on short-term results to the point of interfering with and impeding long-term stability and well-being?"

Here is his answer: "This person would be classified as having *antisocial personality disorder (ASPD) with narcissistic tendencies* or having a *narcissistic personality disorder (NPD) with antisocial tendencies,* depending on that person's primary and secondary motivations."

So, there you have it. If we lay our publicly traded models on the couch, they are diagnosed as either having ASPD with narcissistic tendencies or having NPD with antisocial tendencies, depending on their primary and secondary motives of course. But sociopathic and narcissists all.

ASPD or NPD—which is it? I'm not sure. It simply strikes me as downright squirrelly.

The odometer is clearly the instrument for measuring future advisor-client success. This instrument will serve both the client and the advisory firm well. If we help our clients to make considerable progress in their financial lives, they will reward us with more assets and opportunities to manage wealth and risk. When the odometer is the instrument of choice, everyone can focus on the one thing that matters most—getting people to the destination they've chosen.

### ReSOULution

Commit to the long-term relationship in all systems and behaviors involving the well-being of advisors and their clients. A divided house cannot stand over time and will collapse under the weight of divided interests. Once the journey is measured properly, passengers will sense that instead of being "taken for a ride," they have instead found a copilot for life.

# CHAPTER 3

# The Warring Hand

*Cream rises until it sours.*

—Lawrence Peter

## Insights on the "Conversion" Process

The Saxons, a warring tribe of Europe, were practically compelled to convert to Christianity. They consented on one condition. This condition, they told their converters, would be known only at the time of their baptism. When the warriors were placed under the water as a symbol that their old life was dead, they went under—with the exception of their right arms. They held these out of the water, above their heads. These were their fighting arms. Though they went through the ritual, they were never truly converted. They could not let go of their old warring ways.

I had a conversation with an advisor a while back that left me stunned. Stunned that this sort of conversation was still going on at a wire house after all the bad press of the last few years. I came into contact with this "advisor," whom I will call Dirk, through a referral from a golf buddy who had obtained a LIBOR (London Interbank Offered Rate) loan at a low percentage rate and suggested I call. Following are my notes from two conversations.

## Call 1

"Hi, Dirk. My name is Mitch Anthony. My friend is [so-and-so], who told me about his loan. Are you familiar with who I am?"

"Yeah, I've seen you at the golf club. You wrote a book, didn't you?"

"Actually, I've written eight books. . . ."

Dirk interrupts, "Yeah, yeah . . . Well, anyway, so how much do you want to borrow, and how much do you have in equities and those types of accounts?"

I'm wondering if this is his idea of warming up to a client because it feels more like a chat with a pickpocket as he's going from shaking my hand to reaching for my wallet in a matter of seconds. "Dirk, I think I know where you're going here. You'd like me to move all my accounts to you in order to arrange a loan, but I don't think I'm going to be interested in that arrangement."

"Well, we like to have the whole relationship here. Now, what other assets do you have?"

I'm cringing at his cheapened usage of the term *whole relationship.* "Dirk, I think we might be talking about two different kinds of relationships here. The kind I'm talking about is where you earn my trust and the stewardship of my assets over time."

"Yeah, well, that's fine, but I'll tell you, this is a great deal. I'll have my assistant call you to get the process going."

In spite of Dirk's tactlessness, I continue the call, wanting to investigate the possibility of replacing a 7.5 percent loan on a second property with this much lower rate. We discuss various loan details and the call ends.

## Call 2

Call 2 takes place on Monday morning a few days after Dirk's assistant has called and helped with the application process, during which I discover that I have to remortgage my home to get the quoted rate, something I have no interest in doing. This "detail" never came up during our first conversation.

Call 2 is from Dirk to me. When the caller ID displays his name, I ask my father, a 30-year sales veteran, and my wife if they would like to listen in on Dirk's abrasive and rude approach to financial advice. They nod, and I hit the speakerphone button.

"Mitch here."

"Did you get my message last Friday?"

"Yes, I did."

Dirk replies in a hostile tone. "Well, why didn't your return it? I thought you were into this whole relations . . . relational," he spits the word out like it's poison on his tongue, "thing. We can't build a relationship if you don't return my calls." My father and wife are staring at me in wide-eyed disbelief. They, too, had never witnessed a sales call where the seller opens by chewing out his prospect. It got worse.

"Dirk, I didn't realize when you and I were talking that I would have to remortgage my home in order to get this loan. I just need to get $100,000 to replace a loan I have out at 7.5 percent."

"Well, what's the rate on your house?"

"Six and an eighth, and I'm quite content with it at 15 years. I understand that 3.7 percent is attractive, but that rate fluctuates. Where was this rate four years ago? Seven percent, maybe? I'm comfortable sitting pat at 6 percent."

"I could certainly argue with your philosophy there." Another interesting sales tactic—arguing with your prospect's philosophy, "I've put a lot of people in this loan and they're all very happy they did it." Dirk's tone has now moved toward being condescending and bullying, as if I'm the dumbest dirtball he's ever talked to—after all, "everybody" who has done this is happy, but *you* don't want to. "Oh, by the way, have you read the investing section in the *Journal* this morning? There's a story about Warren Buffett and the fact that he's buying up junk bonds and making a lot of money. What I would suggest is an arbitrage strategy where you borrow at the 3.7 percent and I can put you in a junk bond fund paying 9 percent."

I am dumbfounded at this point. Surely I'm hearing things. I decide to repeat back to Dirk his solicitation so he can hear what it sounds like as an incoming message to a prospect, "So you think that what I ought to do is remortgage my home on a variable-rate loan and put the proceeds into junk bonds?"

The silence hangs for a moment.

Dirk's tone gives away the slightest hint of hesitance. "It's a great arbitrage strategy, and I've got a lot of people taking advantage of it."

"I'll have to think about that, Dirk, and let you know."

End of call.

## Judas Has a New Public Relations Agent

Dirk Black's firm is running a new public relations campaign these days. It tells a story of being all about the client and meeting a client's every need. I'm sure some well-intentioned marketing executives would love to think that the fairy dust of this campaign will affect advisors to behave in this way, but if and when they start holding baptism services for the likes of Dirk Black, they will witness a multitude of hands held high above the water. The Dirk Blacks of this world have no interest in changing their behavior, not after all the top-producer awards they've received acting like a playground bully.

Firms advertise with good intentions. Though well intentioned, they may be ill timed and only serve to fuel a cynical fire burning in the once-burned consumer. The money for advertising would have been better spent on training Dirk Black and his ilk to conduct a more meaningful conversation.

Today's client is not interested in new images about being client centered—they are interested in conversations that demonstrate this ethos. Today's client requires more than service. They want servitude. This servitude expresses itself in a conversation about their life, their needs, and their hopes as opposed to the self-serving conversation about the latest/greatest way to make money. It's their money, and they've exchanged good parts of their lives to get it. The conversation they now expect is about them. Period.

Most financial services firms have figured out that clients now demand and expect an unselfish and facilitating advisor (if new advertising slogans are a reliable indicator), and there is also a swelling awareness of the need for a more qualitative approach in client conversations.

One would have to have been in a coma the past couple of years to miss the televised promise of the new and improved, selfless, even altruistic advisor who can't wait to make your dreams come true. If these campaigns were working, we wouldn't be seeing an ebb of assets leaving many of the businesses advertising as such, would we? What the Madison Avenue gurus failed to interpret was the intense degree of cynicism their ads would provoke from scarred and injured clients as well as observers on the financial services playground.

There is a great gulf between advertisement and advisor. In some places Judas is being advertised as Mother Theresa. Until behaviors are changed advertising dollars are being wasted in publicizing the so-called transformation. Wouldn't these marketing dollars be better spent in processes leading to true transformation in the advisor-client relationship?

Just how great is the gap between advertisement and advisor?

Recently, while discussing the need for a new set of relational and conversational skills for advisors, an editor at a financial services magazine interrupted me to say, "No, that's not what they want to hear. We need to give them new ways to sell." He continued a monologue on selling strategies to itching ears that made me feel like I was in a scene from the movie, *Glengarry Glen Ross*.

The superfluous industry observer assumes wrongly that a new tack is all that is needed. Those who "get it," however, understand that nothing less than a conversion of the very soul of the advisor-client relationship will suffice. It is simply a matter of figuring out who is supposed be served in this relationship. Are we serving the firm at the trough of client portfolios, or are we serving client needs and interests and prospering as a result.

It will take more than a corporate initiative to bridge this gulf—it will take nothing less than a reconstruction of the "advisory process" and a conversion of the salesperson's soul.

## Redefining the Soul of Advice

Such conversions are beginning to take place across the industry as advisors experience the awakening for a new relational dynamic with clients. They are recognizing that a permanent paradigm shift has introduced itself into the client's perspective of a legitimate advisor. The old is giving way to the new. The old way was based on controlling the relationship, convincing the client and competing for attention. This model is based on age-old metaphors of war and gamesmanship. Clients no longer have an interest in being a party to the "game" or in battling with their "advisor."

The new model supplants cooperation for control, conversing for convincing and collaborating for competing. Sound too feminine for you? Welcome to the new world where client interests transcend your own. Time to trade your yin for yang before your business book goes "bang." It is no longer acceptable to attempt to control client decisions. Now advisors must cooperate and partner with clients for answers that serve them in the long run—in other words, they are expected to actually advise, not dictate. No longer do we try to convince people of our assumptions but have real conversations that uncover real needs. No longer do we bad-mouth our competition, because in the end that just speaks ill of the entire industry (think of how some very good, honest firms have suffered because of the sins of the Judases). Those of us who want to succeed now collaborate in any possible way to serve our clients' interests.

## The Evolution of the Advisor

As you can see in Figure 3.1, at the end of the last century, when the rising tide was lifting all boats, the push was on products and the premium was on salesmanship. After market corrections and reports of industry malfeasance were brought to light, the push evolved toward process and the premium was on professionalism. In some cases the push was on appearing professional while continuing to exist as product pushers with initials behind your name. We are now entering the stage of provider evolution, which is moving from a process orientation to a positional orientation, meaning that our emphasis is being properly positioned, for the long term, on the life of our

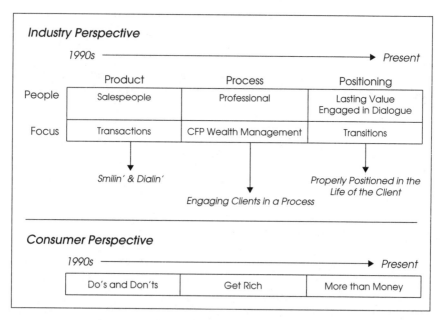

**Figure 3.1    Evolution of Financial Thought**

clients. This is the perpetual value proposition. It does not have a hint of "won and done" to it and requires authentic relational and dialogue skills to accomplish. What this means for the competitive firm is that they must recognize and deal with the fact that the skill sets of salesmanship, recruited and developed in the past, may not pay dividends in the positional marketplace and, in fact, may prove to be detrimental to the long-term client-advisor value proposition.

Intuitive skill sets will become increasingly significant and economically valuable going forward. Such skills include the following:

- The ability to decipher what really matters to *clients*.
- The ability to engage in meaningful dialogues as opposed to boilerplate scripts.
- The ability to find commonality in forming relationships.
- The ability to recognize and improve on emotional competencies.
- The ability to expand relationships by tracking the dynamic nature of clients' lives and interests.
- The ability to "read" emotion and respond appropriately.
- The ability to communicate in visual and emotionally relevant terms.

The competitive tactics of yesteryear have lost their relevance because the competitive field is now about permanence in the life of the client. In the past, the majority of companies created products and pushed those products through advisors. How well those products suited a client's current needs or life became secondary to quotas and, in many cases, mere afterthoughts. The dangerous "middle ground" created by new advertising campaigns is that some companies will continue to do business the same as they always have but will introduce "time to clean up our act" baptismal rituals in an attempt to restore confidence with clients. They will pay lip service to "building relationships," but their warring hand will be noticed by virtue of how quickly the conversation turns to pushing a product.

## The Windfall of Sincerity

Client-centered financial planning and advisory self-transcendence are not the result of an ad campaign but of a purposeful culture that "infects" every product design, every strategic initiative, every process, every advisor training meeting, and every interaction with clients. The warring hand must be converted along with the heart and soul. The convert must come up out of that water knowing that the sins of self-centered financial advice have been washed away.

Recently, while at the practice range of my golf club, I ran into Marv, an independent financial advisor whose business is booming at present. In the past six months, clients with assets totaling $30 million have walked, unsolicited, into his office, many fleeing from relationships with members of Dirk's warring gang. I asked Marv what he owed this windfall of clients to. His answer: "Some of it I owe to the advertising campaigns put out by the offending parties. One client said when he saw the ad and compared it with the behavior of his advisor, he realized just how jaded and demeaning the campaign was. This client lamented that since the firm couldn't keep its original promise to look out for his financial well-being, they answered by making a bigger, more implausible promise.

By contrast, Marv's business plan is quite simple. He asks clients what they have experienced and what they need and gives them what they need, with no compulsion to "move" any particular product. Referral business, Marv assures me, is brisk.

The days of controlling and coercing clients are over. The ways of intimidation and bullying will be left only to those advising on the grade school playground. Dirk is dead. He just doesn't know it yet. As long as clients bend to his "advice," his behavior will be subsidized by their fees, but when they choose to disagree, they will be struck by the warring hand. Once the hand strikes, they will be shocked to their senses and head to the exit, never to return.

Firms must decide whether they want perceptions to change and hope for behaviors to follow or do something about the behavioral standards and let perceptions grow organically.

You can lead a self-centered broker to water, but you can't make him sink.

### ReSOULution

Take time to understand your client's experiences with other financial services providers. There is most likely some skepticism, quite possibly there are seeds of cynicism, and they may even be suffering from a case of "post-traumatic sales syndrome." One important step in restoring trust is in understanding how their views of the industry have been influenced and demonstrating a new and better way through their experience with you.

# CHAPTER 4

# I'm a Numbers Guy

*The great paradox of the twenty-first century is that, in this age of
powerful technology, the biggest problems we face . . . are problems
of the human soul.*

—Ralph Peters

Recently, after giving a speech on filling the relational gap
between clients and advisors, I was approached by a gentleman
named Louie, who informed me, "You know, all this 'touchy-feely'
bit sounds great but I have always been a numbers guy and that is
what I'll always be. I got in the business because I like working with
the numbers and I'm good at it. That's what clients really want."

I walked away from this advisor knowing that he represents a siz-
able segment of the advisor population who are more process than
people oriented and who are more comfortable with a calculator
than they are with a conversation about a client's hopes and needs.
His comment stirred a mix of frustration and introspection in
me—frustration that people like this think they can mimic the
algorithmic functions of a computer and keep clients satisfied;
introspection as to how reach into "Left-Brain Louie" and help him
to see that numbers only serve to help the context from which they
came and will return (i.e., the *life of the client*).

## Numbers Do Matter—But Not in the Way You May Be Expecting: Shortchanged by Numbers

*Clearly then, when someone shows you an economic or financial model that involves mathematics, you should understand that, despite the confident appearance of the equations, what lies beneath is a substrate of great simplification and—sometimes—great and wonderful imagination. Never forget that even the best financial model can never be truly valid because, unlike the physical world, the mental world of securities and economics is much less amenable to the power of mathematics.*

*Many economic journals encourage—or even demand—a faux-rigorous style with multitudes of axioms and lemmas in numbers that tend to be inversely proportional to their efficacy in the real world. . . . Economists seem to have embraced formality and physics envy without the corresponding benefits of accuracy or predictability.*

—Emanuel Derman

Is it possible that we place too much emphasis on the importance of numbers in the advisor-client relationship? Much faith is placed in the gathering and processing of numbers. While numbers gathering and processing are quite integral to the planning and advisory context, it is quite debatable whether they constitute the absolute locus for developing the long-term client relationship. As Derman so eloquently states, from a physicist's point of view, the numbers are quite mutable and unreliable in their ability to either measure or project, and are not nearly as "scientific" as we would like to assert.

## What Numbers Don't Tell Us

Just as we wouldn't commence a client interview with "How are you and how much do you have?," neither should we progress into numbers gathering until the proper emotional context has been established for the work we will do.

There is only so much that the numbers can tell us. They speak only to the material side of the equation. When the popular physicist Brian Greene was asked why he was such a good communicator (unlike his peers), he said, "I don't feel like I understand what I'm doing unless I can form a mental picture of what's going on. If I'm relying on mathematical symbols, I don't feel like I've got the true heart of the science. When it comes to communicating with the public, I take those mental pictures I've developed, strip away the math, and wrap them in a story."

The true science of financial advice is in the story the client tells. This science is best performed by curious individuals and not by printed applications.

We must remember that there is a story behind every number you gather, and in many cases, a very important story. I once heard an accountant give a presentation about the fact that he one day realized there was an important story behind every fact and number on a 1040 tax form. Those who harvest those stories will be in better stead with their clients because, in his mind, the number is not nearly as important as the work and love and sacrifice that produced it.

Numbers and facts tell us what clients have. They do not tell us how hard they worked, what they had to sacrifice, who has and will benefit, who inspired the dream, hardships overcome, pain and joy in the journey, partnerships formed and broken, or amazing breaks and bad fortune navigated in gathering the assets those numbers represent. Behind every success story is a genealogy of events and relationships, one leading into the other, that come together to form an incredibly unique biographical mosaic. Your job, first and foremost—in respect to the price each client has paid—is to uncover as much of that biographical portrait as possible.

## New Numbers for Consideration

One evening as I lay sleepless in my bed, the answer came to me: maybe the way to reach Left-Brain Louie is (ironically) *with numbers*. Louie is partly right: this business is about numbers. But I don't think Louie understands which numbers he should be paying attention to. I'm of the belief that if advisors will pay attention to three specific numbers, they will thrive in the marketplace over the next 10 to 20 years. Here are the three numbers that I believe matter the most:

| | |
|---|---|
| The most important number to building a successful client relationship: | 9/11 |
| The most important number in building a strategy for the future: | 77 |
| The most important numbers in increasing your income: | 40 and 100 |

### 9/11: The Most Important Number to Building Client Relationships

Louie, this may be the most important number you ever discuss with your clients. You'll have to take your eyes off of your software for a moment, however, and look each client in the eye when you ask them this question:

*"How did 9/11 impact your focus and your life?"*

9/11 changed everything, for almost everybody. Hardly a corner of our souls was left untouched. We began to think more in earnest about our families, how precious they are to us, and how quickly our children grow up. We said "I do" to our spouse but lived like we said it to the boss. As a result, we discovered that we don't want to miss out on either the key events or the key years.

*We want to live while we can.* We want some balance in our lives. That one day in September forced us to examine how much of a life we really had. We looked into the mirror of mortality and realized we weren't sure we'd be around tomorrow and knew we couldn't keep relegating all our wishes to a future that may never come. We decided we were done with making a living. We wanted (and want) to make a life.

*We want meaning in our lives.* Priorities shifted like eternal gears on the inside of our hearts. We realized that our time was more important than our money, that our relationships were more important than our results. We realized that our results had better be tied to a sense of meaning and demonstrating to us that we are somehow "making a difference." Many realized that their paychecks were costing more than they were paying us, and many realized how lucky they were to still be receiving a paycheck. We realized that we didn't want to reach the end and have to say, as the poet Friedrich Hebbel once did, "The man I am greets with regret the man I might have been."

9/11 is an important number, Louie. That number is the key that unlocks your clients' priorities—what they want for their family and what they hope for in their life.

### 77: The Most Important Number in Building a Strategy for the Future

Unless you have been bunkered in a demographics cocoon, you have heard that there are a lot of baby boomers and they are headed toward retirement age like a runaway train. More specifically, there are 77 million of them, and in 2005 they began turning 59½ at the pace of one person every seven seconds. The implications for your business going forward are gargantuan in nature. In fact, if you don't prepare yourself and your business strategy, this demographic train will run over you like a kid's nickel laid on the track.

Authors who have been writing about this fat demographic of baby boomers as they move through their various life stages have metaphorically characterized this demographic contingent of boomers as the "pig in the python." This characterization fits because of the disruption these boomers have caused to every traditional juncture of life they have passed through. Institutions affected include no more "company man" along with seven to eight different careers, the antiaging revolution, and now the "new retirementality" (read my book *The New Retirementality* for information on the changing face of retirement).

Don't take this "pig in a python" analogy too far, however, and assume, as some marketers do, that there is some magic key to understanding and capturing this "pig off to market" opportunity. If there is one word that defines the baby boom generation, it is *individuality*. They will not be spoken to as a demographic contingent and will not suffer fools who bring cookie-cutter solutions. These 77 million people want an advisor who treats them as the unique individual they are and who is willing to take the time to find out how it is that this individual plans to "self-actualize," to borrow from Abraham Maslow. So individual in their bent are these 77 million boomers that I prefer to refer to them as 77 million individual strips of bacon in a python.

The individual conversation you have with these people will eventually work its way to the numbers; if it's starting there, you'll lose them. The conversation they are interested in first and foremost is about the lifestyle they want to live and the dusty dreams they want to pull off the shelf. These 77 million don't consider the age of 65 as old and are not interested as a whole in shuffleboard, condo association warfare, and spending all their time in an RV staring at their growing navel (think Jack Nicholson in *About Schmidt* here).

They are still interested in work (just not as much), and in making sure it's work they enjoy (according to an AARP survey, at least 70 percent want to die with their boots on). They are interested in getting educated in new areas and pursuing personal growth. They are interested in investing their talents, time, and resources in activities they know will "make a difference." They are not interested in a life of total leisure and early-bird specials. They know a life of total ease is one step from a life of disease. They want to plan a life where they are free to pursue what is on the inside of them screaming to get out. If that conversation sounds too squishy to you, you may have to hire someone skilled at conversation and head to the back office.

On the numbers side, they are interested in how they can start taking income now or on their 59½ birthday. They want to use their money ASAP to cause that life vision we just talked about to emerge. So you may have to abandon that rusty old accumulation spiel and get versed in an "income for life" dialogue if you want to be in business 10 years from today.

I'm getting the feeling that I'm sending your right brain into tilt right now, so I'm going to cross back over to the quantitative hemisphere for one last set of numbers you may want to look at.

### 40–100: The Most Important Numbers for Increasing Your Income

A question I have been posing to scores of financial service firms for the last few years is this: "What is the average percentage of clients' assets entrusted to your average advisor?" I have heard answers ranging from abysmal single digits as a low to 40 percent as a high. There are only two reasons I can think of for clients not to bring more assets to you, Louie: (1) You don't have the products or services needed to assist clients with 100 percent of their assets, and (2) they don't trust you with any more than 40 percent.

I have made a study of advisors whose clients typically entrust 100 percent of their assets to their custody and management. I have noted major differences in how they conduct their business, but most notably the foundation from which they conduct their client relationships. Following are a few of those differences.

**100 Percent Advisors Conduct Dialogues, Not Monologues.**   A monologue starts with asking a question you know the answer to and using the anticipated answer as a launching pad to sell whatever it was you were going to sell before you ever asked the question. The question is used as a tool of manipulation. Think clients have missed the industry scandal headlines of the past three years and don't have their antennae tuned to sales "tactics"? Think again.

A *dialogue* begins with a question that is designed to discover who the client is, what they really need, and where their hopes lie. You can engage in a dialogue only if you are comfortable entering a conversation where you don't know what their answer will be. You will need the lucidity and agility to "go with the flow" until the real needs are uncovered and a real "connection" is made. This requires some intuitive skill Louie, and I'm afraid that word *intuitive* might be just enough to send you over the edge and running back to your desk to huddle up with your spreadsheets.

The reason 40 percent advisors prefer monologues is that their business is centered on moving products. The reason 100 percent advisors prefer dialogues is that their business in centered on helping clients make progress in their financial lives. They engage in financial life planning with life at the center of every dialogue. They understand that the context that drives everything is what the client wants to happen with their life. It is the heart and soul of why this industry even exists. Operating outside of that life context in the outer periphery of "moving products" leads to hollow, empty relationships and hollow, empty images of oneself.

**100 Percent Advisors Put Their Faith in Building Quality Relationships; Others Lean on Outperforming Some Set of Numbers They Cannot Control.**   A lot of numbers guys love to show clients how they can beat the returns of the S&P, funds in its peer group, or the manager down the block. The pitfall is that the relationship with the client now hinges on keeping promises that should never be made in the first place. How much control does an advisor have over industry indices and competitors' performances? None. Why build relationships on sinking sand or swelling waves that have the power to sink you or wash you away when you could build them on the quality of your relationships?

Sounds like a no-brainer to me. Or, at least a right-brainer.

Dan is an advisor for a major wire house in a small city in the upper Midwest. There are only two national firms represented in this town, so it didn't take Dan long to figure out who his competition was. Dan is quick to inform you that he is a "relationship guy," that he invests the time getting to know his clients and knowing what is going on in their lives. His competitor is the quintessential "quant" or numbers guy.

Dan tells the story of meeting the young advisor who had moved to town representing a third wire house and was attempting to steal away clients from both Dan and the other advisor. The proselytizing competing advisor came to Dan one day and asked in exasperation, "What is it with you and your clients!?" Dan asked him what his interest was.

The advisor explained, "As you may know, I have been calling every person in town to get my business off the ground. When I call your competitors' clients, they talk my ear off and I've landed a number of major accounts. When I call your clients, they refuse to even have a conversation with me, and more than a few have just hung up the phone in my ear!"

Dan laughed (and breathed an affirmative sigh of relief). He told the young advisor that he worked hard at building relationships and that he suspected that was the reason he wasn't getting through.

Dan had shrunk the dynamic distance between his client's hopes and needs and his products and services by investing himself in the relationship-building side of the business. That dynamic distance had now contracted to the point that Dan's client's felt a sense of partnership with him, and they were offended when another party tried to interject their presence between them.

The epilogue to this story is that Dan's new competitor was so impressed that Dan's company encouraged him to operate this way instead of pounding on him to "move product" that he left his firm within the year and joined Dan's firm.

**To the 100 Percent Advisor the Client, Not the Money, Is the Client.**    These are the advisors whose clients entrust all their assets to them because they have made it crystal clear that their chief interest is who the client is, not just what they have. Look at most discovery forms used by major firms: less than 10 percent qualitative inquiry and 90 percent or more of quantitative inquiry (or intrusion, as the case may be). It gives one the feeling that he is a safety deposit box and once the combination is found, it's "game over."

My friend and coauthor, Scott West, satirically stated, "The other day I heard a doctor talking about how pleased he was with the information he had gathered on his patient. 'I've got X-rays on about 40 percent of his body, from the hips on down, and feel like I can really do a job of helping him.'"

Scott's wit cuts at the quick of just how much we can do for clients who have put 40 percent of their trust in us. Paradoxically, they will never invest 100 percent with us until we invest 100 percent in understanding them and working in their best interests.

At conventions I often hear advisors describing clients in conversation—"I've got this $2 million guy," "I have this $800,000 executive"—and I wonder how these clients would take to being characterized as a number. Actually, being characterized as an amount of money is worse than being characterized as a number. We don't take offense to being classified with nine digits by the Social Security administration, but our advisor referring to us by our account balance is another matter altogether. Such references to the client are symptomatic of the fact that, to the 40 percent advisor, the money *is* the client. The 100 percent advisor knows the client is a "who" and not a "what" and forms a partnership with the person and not the account.

I've probably been a little long-winded on the numbers here and taken a bit more time than the Louie left-brainers would care for (that's a downside to us "relationship" guys). My guess is that Louie's crowd could go on doing business the way they always have, engage in same conversations, do the same analyses, and utilize the same business strategy. But they had better be careful. There are a lot of "relationship guys" out there, and they've got their eyes on their clients. A lot of those clients are hungry to talk, to discover, to plan a life and *then* figure out a way to pay for it. They may want an advisor who will invest some time in them.

Louie can keep doing what he's always done, but I've got a sneaking suspicion that his days are numbered.

## ReSOULution

Understand that behind every number is a story to be told. This industry must begin to recruit and develop people who are masters of dialogue and gathering important stories.

A leading executive in the industry recently made this sage observation, "I wonder if we don't need to go back to the drawing board

*(continued)*

on the type of personality we hire. We hired these number crunchers who excel at processes and are awkward with people and as we see the need for a different type of advisor, it feels like we're trying to teach fish to walk."

There is a story that created the number(s) on the client forms before you and stories of where those numbers will apply down the road. The numbers describe only material content. Stories from their life describe the context. Without understanding the context that drives the clients' emotions and life, you can never grasp the meaning behind the means. Advisors for life understand that narratives reveal much more than numbers ever could.

# 5

# A New Level of Integrity Beyond Disclosure

*Honesty is always an alternative.*

—Bob Moomey

Bob sat with me at my kitchen counter with forms and small piles of small-print spread out before us. Bob, an insurance specialist, recently joined the team of my accountant, who has been helping me manage my personal and business financial affairs for over 25 years. Before us, waiting for signatures, were applications for three products, a disability policy, a term-life policy for key people in my business, and a variable universal life split-dollar policy.

I like to know the stories of people I do business with so I asked Bob where he was from and how he got involved in the insurance business. After he shared a short biography, I asked how he liked the insurance business. He said he liked it fine, but I thought I picked up a slight reticence in his tone and eyes. I asked him what it was that he found difficult in this business.

"I feel like I'm wrestling with my conscience every day in this business. The company is always telling us to do what is best for the client but puts me in situations every single day where I have to deal with the temptation of doing otherwise. I'm fairly young in this business but I don't know how long I can last. It goes against the values of my faith and upbringing."

I asked him for an example.

"When I was being trained, the guy who trained me would sit down with a client and show him his fund choices for a particular product. One hundred percent of the time he steered the client to one fund. I asked him why he didn't steer some people to the fund that had no up-front cost and he said, 'Because I get paid 3.5 percent when they "choose" this fund.' And that's the way it is right there. How do you reconcile yourself with that? You have to make a living, but you're supposed to do what is *best* for the client, not what is tolerable, or whatever you can pull by unwitting clients."

"Bob," I told him, "I might have the answer for you. It will make you nervous at first but will set you free in the end. It's called *absolute transparency*. It's where you lay your cards on the table and demonstrate transparency about how you are being compensated for everything you do."

He looked at me quizzically, like you would at a lunatic running in the street yelling "Save the whales!"

"Funny," I said, "how the insurance industry hasn't yet caught up with car dealers on this issue. Ever been to one of those car lots that don't play games with you? They tell you what they paid for a vehicle and what they want for it. They build a profit center in the back end of the business with their service center because they haven't sabotaged it on the front end with compensation games. How does it feel to be in a business that ranks below car dealers in transparency?"

"I've never thought of it that way, but you're right," Bob answered.

"Another question you might want to ask yourself," I offered, "is how long can the industry prosper playing these hide-and-seek games in the shadows of small print?"

"Or, how long can I last being asked to play out this mixed message," Bob offered.

"Just for fun and illumination, "I asked, "I want to ask you to do something you may never have been asked to do before. I want you to write down on a piece of paper what you are being paid for all three of these products that are sitting before us. I want it in real dollars, not just percentage points. Both the up-front and the trailing fees."

Bob blushed like Macy's Christmas tree.

It's okay," I assured him, "I'm not going to chase you off."

We walked through the commission and fees on the variable universal life (VUL), disability, and term policies. When he was finished explaining every last penny he would make and how long he would make it, he stopped and seemed to be holding his breath for my response.

"Bob," I said, "I don't have a problem with any of it, and I'll tell you why. I understand the value you and my accountant bring into my life with these products. The VUL will help my income needs and tax issues later in life. That's well worth the price. The disability policy safeguards my family in case anything unexpected ever does happen, and the term policy safeguards my business, the people who work for me and the clients we serve. I understand the value and I'd rather see you make this income than someone who didn't understand the intricacies of my situation. You see, Bob, the practice of absolute transparency forces you as the provider to put more emphasis on the front end of the conversation and to truly establish a real-life context for the product being sold. If you do that correctly and with sincerity, you'll have little resistance on compensation, as you have just witnessed."

"Wow," he breathed a big sigh of relief, "that feels great."

## Under the Surface

"Bob," I asked, "how many times have you suspected that the client was sitting there wondering what you were going to make out of this, and you were wondering what they were wondering?"

"Every time," he answered, "every single time."

"Bob, I can think of only two reasons you wouldn't want to do this: (1) you don't believe in your company or (2) you don't believe you personally bring enough value to my situation. With absolute transparency," I assured him, "you remove that tension and potential for distrust from your life. No more mystery. No more hiding behind jargon and fine print. And when you're finished, you can invite the client to shop around and see that you are competitive."

"After hearing this," he said, "I doubt if many clients would want to go elsewhere."

"What are the odds of the next person being absolutely transparent?" I asked, "Now the client knows something about your competition that your competitor isn't aware of." Truth does have its competitive advantages.

## An Axe to the Roots

One night I was out having dinner with a group of advisors who, for understandable reasons, were lamenting the increasing pressure and scrutiny upon their businesses by the powers that be. One of the people at the table offered a lament for his fellow advisors, throwing his hands in the air and exclaiming, "What are *we* to do?"

I was instantly transported to a sermon I heard a decade ago about the days when John the Baptist was making a stir over the hypocrisy of his culture and contemporaries. No one was spared his scourging tirades. His candor would eventually cost him his head as he chastised Herod for his adulterous relationship with his brother's wife. In the story, he is baptizing followers in a river; he shouts to his audience, "Bring deeds worthy of repentance." He sensed that perhaps some were coming for the cleansing ritual without doing a thorough inventory of their personal behavior. He is approached by three men, one a soldier, one a tax collector, and one a common citizen, who all asked him, "What are *we* to do?" Interestingly enough, John's prescriptions for transparency for all three of them centered on their behavior with money:

> To the soldier: "Be content with your wages and don't use your position and authority to extort."
>
> To the tax collector: "Collect no more than what is just and due."
>
> To the common citizen: "Practice generosity with those less fortunate."
>
> He finished his admonition with the admonition: "Now is the axe laid to the root. . . ."

A day of judgment has already dawned on the financial services industry, and the axe has only begun to strike. Regarding the growing cynicism and judgment within the gargantuan baby boomer contingent, industry consultant Larry Klein writes, "The older ones were the hippies and campus protesters. It's in their blood to distrust the establishment: big securities firms, big insurance companies, any they believe might be associated with the 'man,' seeking to rip them off."

Bogus stock recommendations and the dot-bomb, mutual fund after-hours dalliances, whoring investment banks, and post-traumatic stress stories on specific abuses around products like variable annuities served to hasten the sharpening of the axe that now falls.

Judgment is already upon us.

This judgment will continue until it has satisfactorily scrutinized compensation on both the value of the trade and the transparency of the exchange. The hidden things will be brought to light and every man's work will be made manifest.

Two forms of repentance will accompany the imposing judgment. The first form will come before the floodlight, and the second form will come after. The "before" repentance will be those who choose to demonstrate "absolute transparency" before their clients. These professionals will come out the winners because their repentance was an act of the heart.

The "after" repentance will be the grudging and bitter response to new rules of total disclosure. These souls will not be long for the industry, and their clients will be willing tenants of the "before" crowd.

If you doubt that this day and drama is coming, look to the portending events in the United Kingdom in the past decade, where total disclosure laws have reduced the financial advisor community, by some estimates up to 80 percent. Amazing what becomes of the pestilence when the bright light of judgment appears. But good people will be swallowed up in the judgment as well as the pestilence. Good people with good intentions who simply lacked the courage to demonstrate absolute transparency. The United Kingdom's advisor experience, I fully expect, foreshadows our own. Informed and once-burned consumers will settle for nothing less than a fair and transparent reckoning.

## Your Value Proposition

Why should anyone choose to do business with you over another provider? 'Because of the kind of relationship I bring" is the answer I expect to hear from most advisors. What will become of that relationship if your client finds out, before you tell them, how and what you are being paid?

Once the cards are on the table regarding what you make and how you make it, you will find yourself naked and blushing if you are nothing more than a product purveyor. Changing the descriptor on your business card to "Wealth Manager" won't change any client's opinion of the value they have or have not received in the past 10 years.

In a truly democratic fashion I want to shine the light of emotional reality on the value proposition of commissions, assets under management, and fee only services. I hope that advisors in all three camps are equally challenged to search for a deeper, more perpetual value proposition.

### Commissions

In the venue of absolute transparency you simply reveal what you get paid. If it is fair, the client will be satisfied. If it is not fair, they will go elsewhere. If it is unfair across the industry, downward price pressure will make the correction until it is fair. Most people are reasonable and understand that, as a provider, you have to make a living. They just don't care to see inequitable gaps between value received and price paid. Kind of like the congregation in a church in the ghetto who were offended when their preacher showed up driving a brand new Lexus.

As a consumer, I don't have a problem with reasonable commissions, and I don't believe that just because someone is receiving a commission that they are trying to exploit me for their paycheck. Some of the most upstanding, moral, and trustworthy individuals I know on this planet are being paid commissions.

I work with one advisor who is one of the last of the old breed of "stock pickers." He charges me full commission rates for his picks. Are these rates high? They are sometimes 50 times higher than I once paid at a discount (online) brokerage. I managed to lose a lot of money executing $7 per trade rates and came to understand the value of making good, well-researched picks. Do I wish my full-service guy charged less? Sure, I'll always settle for less paid out, but I am content with the value I am getting, and the results bear it out. I happen to feel that we may be in a flat market for a long time and that the ability to pick out the right companies is at a premium right now. I also have an understanding with this advisor: if you haven't bought it for your own portfolio, don't bother calling me.

A final note on commissions: If a realtor came to me and said, "I'll give you a choice—pay me 5 percent up front or 1 percent a year for every year they live in the house," I'll take the up-front commission every time. This leads us to the value proposition within assets under management.

### Assets under Management

Why should you get paid more because I made more? Why should you be paid more for making the same allocation decision regarding $2 million that you would for $1 million? I'm not asking these questions to say it is wrong that you are paid on assets under management, but to see if you can answer me without blinking. If you hesitate, you are, yourself, doubting the credibility of the value proposition of assets under management. What happens when people figure out that there are only so many allocation scenarios and that they can get the same one you suggested from Vanguard for half of what you charge? How will you then vindicate your value proposition?

There must be real and perpetual value in a scenario where a constant fee is charged. We do not want to arouse "middle-man rage" in clients. This is what you begin to feel on toll roads where every dollar you drop simply buys a lift of the gate from a municipality or state that probably has paid for the road a thousand times already but continues to charge you because it can.

### Fee Only

A veteran executive in the mutual fund industry told me the following: "I was looking for the purest value proposition with an advisor and settled on the 'fee-only' approach. I was happy with the transparency and the straightforward approach but noticed that my satisfaction began to diminish over time. They were charging me the same thing year after year but had provided the bulk of the value in the first year."

If you charge a client $250 to tell them they need term insurance and then they go down the street to buy it, did they come out ahead? The answer is "yes" if you saved them from buying something they didn't need at a rate they shouldn't pay. But the answer is "no" if they already knew that coming in.

The fee-only value proposition, like the assets under management proposition, requires the demonstration of perpetual value in order to succeed over time. If you are advertising as "fee only," it is also important to reveal every fee you are paid and how much you are paid. I have met a number of advisors who advertise as "fee only" but seem to blur the borders of the things they get paid on.

No matter what business model you have chosen, transparency will work in your and your client's behalf. Dana, a local advisor who has taken this message to heart and is transparent in all his financial discussions with clients and prospects offers this:

> I've grown accustomed to this surprised look that says "Nobody ever told me that before!" This conversation also takes away the nagging thought in the back of their minds: "Is this solution being offered because of the money he'll make?" With a transparent dialogue, you are immediately proving your own trustworthiness, and people want to work with someone they can trust. Once they know they can trust you, they don't have to look elsewhere. This is a relief to them. I believe that if you are afraid to reveal how much you're making, you are not confident about the value you bring to the table.

The only way to walk confidently is to know that you do, indeed, bring greater value. Transparency about how you get paid and how the industry works is, in and of itself, a greater value when you look at how many advisors camouflage their sources of income.

What other greater values, besides absolute integrity, can you legitimately sell to your clients that will retain perpetual value? One advisor puts it this way:

> I'm no different than you or anyone else in business. When I'm paid, I pay attention, and I believe people are willing to pay you to pay attention to them. The key is to follow through on the promise of paying attention. They do not, however, want to "pay through the nose" or want to find out that the security guard has fallen asleep at the monitor.

The best advisors know that the time has passed where one could hide behind small print and use fancy and sophisticated jargon to paint a picture of value that was nothing more than a veneer. The time has come to demonstrate real and lasting value with an open or forthright spirit. The best advisors cannot afford to go along with the ways of the past because, once a client becomes informed on compensation, they will look with a jaundiced eye at all the good you may have done. Your previous commitment and sincerity will have been largely wasted simply because you did "business as usual." Consider this:

What if you hired a guide to an exotic locale and told them to line up the best hotels, the best meals, and the best excursions.

You then went on the trip and had a wonderful time, but upon returning found out that every place you went—the hotels, the restaurants, the excursions—had all paid this guide to steer you to their place of business. You had paid them to represent you with an objective eye and to ensure that you had a great experience. Even though your experience was good, it is now tainted because you realize it was his own interests that were really being represented, not yours.

He may have been a wonderful guide, but it no longer matters.

## Life in the Light

I came home to find this e-mail from Bob, whose conversation I opened this chapter with:

> I have already used at least a half-dozen times the advice you gave regarding the full disclosure of what I am making on a given product and the response has been exactly what you said it would be. The undercurrent of not trusting that you as the advisor are really working for my best interest just fades away once I share that information. THANK YOU!!

Bob now knows. The truth is not only an option; it is a powerful force to be reckoned with. Better to be the person doing the reckoning than to be reckoned with by your clients. When you are the one bringing truth to the top of the table, you will find that the truth will set you free.

### ReSOULution

Live in a place of absolute clarity, where nothing is completed in the shadows, where you can look every man and woman in the eye and know that the trade is worth it because of the integrity and care that you bring. Choose transparency for the simple reason that it is the right thing to do and because it allows you a clear sense of confidence in yourself and your value.

# CHAPTER 6

# A New Value Proposition

*The most important question to ask on the job is not "What am I getting?" The most important question to ask on the job is "What am I becoming?" It is hard to keep that which has not been obtained through personal development. . . . What you become directly influences what you get.*

—Jim Rohn

Last fall I was asked to speak at a financial planner's client appreciation banquet that was close enough to home that I asked my wife to come along. The prefacing comments, delivered by financial planner Marty Kurtz, were in one of the most touching, transparent, and moving speeches I have ever witnessed.

My wife and I were deeply moved by the utterly honest, from-my-soul-to-yours message Marty shared with his clients. What he did was lay out his value proposition with as much candor and concern as you could ever hope to hear from your financial advisor.

First, the transparent truth: Marty began by telling the 135 clients in the room what it was that he did that really mattered. He said, "I do asset allocation and planning reviews for all of you. And basically you are all invested in fairly the same way with different allocations. To be honest, you could probably find 20 other advisors within 10 miles of us who could all do a good job in these areas. We do those things and try to do them well but that is not what I am all about."

Marty then went on to describe what his "real" value proposition was: "Our financial planning center was opened because the world is more complex and we're all just one minute away from chaos and what we do is a risk management strategy for our lives." Marty went on to tell them that he believed they came to him for two reasons:

1. Perspective
2. Direction and understanding

And to emphasize the second point he accentuated his own purpose by saying, "The real value I want to bring to you is to know what really matters to you and to be a part of that."

During Marty's presentation, he did something else I had never seen before. He played a slide show of the work that his daughter had undertaken with preschool children. He told of her mission in life and introduced her, to the applause of his clients. Marty wasn't acting the part of the all-knowing financial planner but the wise advisor who chose to be real and share something significant from his life with his clients. His clients were not only visibly touched but quite aware of why Marty and his fine staff were with them.

Marty's client gathering felt more like a family reunion than a client meeting, and Marty had no doubt succeeded in building a community, not just a business.

Steve, like other advisors who have utilized the tools I'm talking about here, says that he has seen good relationships become great relationships and that he has seen referrals into the family that were not forthcoming before because the chief topic at hand was money and its management.

"Now we're talking about their lives first, and they say things like, you know, my brother and his wife have a health situation that is causing a lot of stress. I'm going to recommend that they talk to you so they can go through this same process. This has been so helpful for us."

Enlarging the context for the relationship to be focused first on life alerts your clientele that you are in a different business than the average financial professional and that as they encounter other loved ones navigating money/life issues, they will think of your unique expertise in this arena.

Great financial planners—true financial life planners—don't engage in games of pretense. They don't hang their hat on functions and processes that are a dime a dozen in the marketplace. Financial life planners connect at a deeper level than allocation or even financial strategies can ever hope to touch. They connect at the heart. The value proposition that connects with the heart is not easily threatened or broken. There is just not that much competition out there that gets this point.

## A New Value Proposition

Mark called me asking if I had any ideas about how to generate a more positive and more enjoyable conversation for his annual meetings with clients. I asked him what was wrong with the conversations he was currently engaged in. He answered, "I am so weary of this 'returns' discussion. 'How much did I make? How does it compare to this and that index?' It's like the movie *Groundhog Day*, where the same thing keeps happening over and over again."

I don't know if it was the coffee I was sipping or my inability to restrain my opinion that caused me to ask Mark this question, "How do you suppose *that* conversation got started, and *how do you suppose this context was created for your relationships?*"

I wanted him to do some serious soul-searching about the monster he had created in his value proposition to clients. Every conversation he had with clients affirmed the fact that he had brought his practice under the *tyranny of returns* because, at some point, in developing this relationship he sold the client on a value proposition that he could do better than the indexes and, most assuredly, better than that advisor down the street. Now he was living under the tyrannical rule of that naive promise.

I assured Mark that once he accepted responsibility for the tone, focus, and content of his current conversations, he could make a quantum leap into more positive conversational territory. But this quantum leap comes with a price, the price being that one must first admit that the idea of building a value proposition to clients based on factors beyond your control is a foolish idea.

Let me illustrate with an analogy:

> I have a new service I would like to offer to you. I am a certified weather advisor. Here is my business proposal: Bring me your calendar for the following year and circle the dates that you want to have outings—a picnic, a ball game, or maybe a

short vacation. What I will do is tell you whether it is going to
be rainy or sunny on that particular day. Is anyone interested?

You're beginning to wonder if the bulb on my front porch is
flickering. So you think I've bought some property on the edge
of sanity, do you? Perhaps you could tell me what the difference is
between my proposition and the one you're making to clients that
offers to beat someone's or some index's returns?

Hey, I've got an idea—how about building a business, life,
career, and well-being on circumstances completely beyond our
control and then sitting down at the end of every year to demonstrate to clients how we have failed. Now *that* is insane. Sounds like
a formula for stress for all parties involved. It almost makes my
weather advice service sound doable.

Do you think that if a client who did business with my weather
advisory service came to me upset because they had scheduled a
picnic and it had rained would be consoled and satisfied by my saying, *"Yes, but it only rained half an inch. Everywhere else it rained three
fourths of an inch. Historically, it only rains on that date one in seven
years. I think we did the right thing."*

All my clients know is that their plans got rained on and I sold
them on sunshine. We are simply delivering an inferior value proposition and having the wrong primary conversation with clients,
especially in the annual review conversation.

Mark said it took some time for him to be able to segue his
value proposition to the life side of the ledger because he had done
such a good job of selling himself as a "wealth manager" that they
expected nothing more than financial expertise from him. Once
he began to approach the topic with conviction, he saw a change.
"I simply began to say, 'You and I both know that you've got a lot
of your life wrapped up in this money and what happens with it. I
have determined that to do the best job I can do and for us to have
the kind of partnership we need to have, I need to know the stories of what challenges and opportunities you face year in and year
out. There are a lot of people out there who can manage assets, but
there aren't a lot of them who can do that and make sure it fits with
your life as it changes. This is the kind of relationship I'm about
building with you and all my clients.'"

Mark's clients are touched by his candor and sincerity and
are keen to tell friends who have struggled with other financial

professionals about the unique relationship they have found with Mark. It's not all that difficult to stand out with the money/life value proposition in today's marketplace, if it's done with sincerity.

## Running Out of Gas

What if you walked into a car lot and the first thing they asked you was "How many miles are you getting per gallon?"

You answer, "20."

They say, "I've got a vehicle here that will get you 22."

You buy it. And find out that it got you only 20 even though the sticker said it would get 22. Another dealer approaches you and hears your story and says, "I've got a car here that says it will get you 25 but in actuality will get you 23." You then buy that car.

My question to you as an advisor is this: *Why in the world would you want to be in the "miles per gallon" business?* If you are hanging your professional hat on your ability to get better returns on investments, you have fallen into an inferior value trap that can be sabotaged every quarter by an earnings report and by competitors' sales pitches of better mileage. Move your conversation to a higher level by asking the following questions first:

- Where do you want to go in this vehicle?
- Who is going with you?
- Why do you want to go there?
- How important is safety?

After you hear the answers to all these questions, it may become quite apparent that the best solution for this client is a Chevy Suburban, and you are going to say, "Given your destination, your passengers, and your concerns, I would recommend the Suburban, but you need to prepare yourself for the reality of getting 12 to 14 miles per gallon. Are you willing to make that trade-off? If not, you'll be annoyed by the fact that others are getting better mileage even though they have made trade-offs with both safety and comfort."

You just moved your conversation from a commodity you can't really control to an advisory role tied to the journey instead of the mechanics of the situation.

## Brown Can Do It for You

On a recent airplane trip, I sat next to an executive with United Parcel Service (UPS), who explained how his company transformed itself from a package delivery company to a "supply chain management" firm. It all hearkens back to the big picture. "Delivering packages, we soon learned, is a commodity," this executive informed me. "Once it becomes a commodity, it enters into the pricing war zone. Using our powers of observation, we noted that we delivered packages by the millions for thousands of companies and realized we knew more, by virtue of our expansive viewpoint, than most all of them about supply chain management. We decided to start selling our expertise instead of relying on the commodity for our well-being."

By appealing to the context of the commodity it served, UPS transformed its business into a big-picture strategic business that sells advice as an entrée to the commodities it delivers. That's a whole different ball game, and one that financial advisory firms would do well to emulate.

Why would you make the fluctuation of markets, return on investments, and indexes beyond your control the foundation of your business success? It's a naive, callow idea, and annual and unpleasant client conversations only attest to that fact. A gentler way of stating this opinion about beating indexes or benchmarks set by others was recently offered in a speech I attended by Jean Marie Eveillard, the president and founder of First Eagle Funds, who said, "If you are going to engage in index hugging, be prepared for the fact that the odds are that you will do slightly less than the index and thereby give your clients a reason to no longer need you."

*Merci*, Monsieur Eveillard. Your opinion is much more qualified than mine on such quantitative issues.

In a moment I will introduce to you a conversation that will begin to remove this unnecessary stress from your life, turn the annual review into a joyride, and move your clients' focus to the place it belongs—on making progress in their lives by proper utilization of their resources.

## Enough about You—Let's Talk about Them

The financial services industry has come to a place where there is a need for new measures to meet a rising realization and awareness— *having more money does not guarantee living a richer life*. If the financial services industry fails to respect this fact of fiscal consciousness and the rising boomer awareness around it, a subculture within the industry is going to rise up and corral the most affluent markets. This subculture of intuitively skilled planners and advisors recognizes the shortcomings of money-maniacal conversations, the need for holistic context and the insatiable boomer need to "make their life count." *The tacit—and soon to become vocal at the societal level—demand this generation will place on this industry is for a more integrative experience around their money, one that gives equal weighting to account balances and balance in life, equal weighting to their sources of means and sense of meaning.*

Don't get me wrong. This is a financial conversation, and I recognize that this is a financial business. I am simply suggesting that the client is ready for a conversation with an advisor who understands that quality of life, not money, is the core issue. Money—where to invest it, how to plan around the financial issues—is the peripheral concern that gets its relevance only from the life issues it serves. How do we go about measuring our performance on this new agenda of "money for life"? Obviously, measuring how our portfolio did against the Dow or any index won't come close. Neither will the value proposition of simply matching those indexes. What the heck do I care about an index and how I did against it? I want to make progress with my life and dreams. My proposal is for a more relevant measure that gives us an idea of how we are doing against our vision and progress toward a better, more balanced life—a measure that tells us how we are performing against our hopes and dreams.

Also relevant to this conversation is how you measure your success in this business compared to how your client measures her success. AUM (assets under management) is so limited. I may have $600,000 in investable assets but $4 million in net worth. Like the accountant who discovered that a client he charged $500 per year for a tax return had $54 million in assets, we miss the greater opportunity to help clients by focusing on their liquid means (assets) instead of the meaning they hope to achieve (the return on their life, or ROL). Open the soul to what the money *is intended for,* and the wallet will not be far behind.

Ironically, the advisor who understands true affluence focuses on life issues *and* is positioned to service assets—the liquid, the illiquid, and those in various stages of transition between the two.

The advisor operating on the lower standard of AUM misses the bulk of the opportunity because of this shortsighted and opportunistic devotion to liquid and immediately investable assets. As you can see in Figure 6.1, the financial tree of life can only remain alive if its roots are strong.

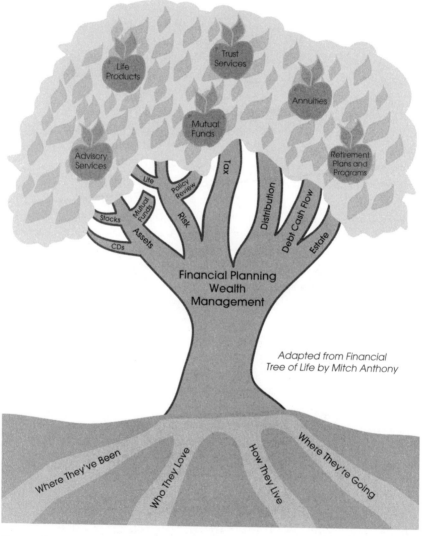

**Figure 6.1   The Financial Tree of Life**

## How We Measure Progress

For the past year, I've lost sleep over this entire perplexing riddle of what defines progress. Here are some clues that can lead us to an answer:

- The unpleasant annual review.
- The futility of measuring success with factors that are beyond our control.
- The real, living intentions that people have for their money that do not get evaluated properly.

After that year of losing sleep, I am ready to offer an answer to this riddle! I've developed a template for the annual review called *THE P.R.O.F.I.T. STATEMENT*™. The example in Table 6.1

**Table 6.1  P.R.O.F.I.T. Statement™ (Progress Report on Financial Intentions to Date) for Mitch and Debbie Anthony**

| Your Life Concerns | Progress Report |
|---|---|
| Concern about aging parents | Both parents continue to receive annuitized payouts on "parental pensions." Principal is stable and payout is guaranteed for parents' lifetimes. Insurance policy is in place for long-term care. Asset transfer has taken place to subsidize parents' new home. Investment has been addressed in parents' will. |
| College education for children: Nic, Sophia and Alec | 529 plans for Nic, Sophia, and Alec all increased in the last calendar year and are 40%, 25%, and 20% of the way, respectively, toward their goal. Following are each child's contributions to their funds: Nic: $876; Sophia: $223; Alec: $235 |
| **Your Goals** | |
| Your charitable giving | Created monthly income stream for the ONE LIFE charity. Created monthly income stream for three missionary causes (Fishers of Men, One More International, and Rescantado Vidas in Costa Rica) |
| Expose children to charitable giving | Established a donor-advised fund compositely for all four children (Nate, Nic, Sophia, and Alec) with "seed money" of $25,000. Each child will "direct" a donation of $400 per year to the charity of their choice. |

illustrates how this template worked for a conversation between my wife, me, and our advisor. This conversation will do a better job of getting to the heart of the matter.

In our annual review, our advisor first and foremost is now having a conversation with us about issues that are well within our parameters of control—what did we do to address the concerns and goals we articulated?

## Understanding True Wealth

True Wealth and the measures of it cannot be achieved or articulated through a financial discussion trapped in a vacuum of numbers and projections and comparisons to benchmarks. True wealth is achieved by understanding the context of your clients' lives, whether it be freedom to spend time with loved ones, the desire to explore a life-long dream, the need to do work they've longed to do, or freedom to leave a philanthropic mark in the world.

There is not a calculator or quantitative analysis in the world that can pave the path to that sort of wealth and we cannot measure it with numbers. Put that index-comparing, stress-inducing, extraneous annual review conversation out to pasture, or at the very least, give it second billing. Turn that annual review into a pleasant experience by conversing on the topic that really matters; that is, "Did we make progress toward your (our) goals?" I'm guessing this conversation will work better than one with the benchmarks, if for no other reason but that it puts us back in control of the situation.

### ReSOULution

Help clients become more aware of the context their money serves: quality of life. Life does not exist in the abundance of things. The thing we want is the abundance of life. Speak to this end, draw it out, make it the bull's-eye that you aim for in each client case you manage.

# CHAPTER 7

# A New Standard for Practice

## PRACTICING WORLD-CLASS WEALTH CARE

*The only interest worth considering is what is in the best interest of the patient.*

— Dr. William Mayo

I suspect that the time has come for a new metaphorical standard to represent the business of providing financial advice. The metaphor that defines the industry also defines your client's experience. Because of the focus on risk and reward, the industry unwittingly fell prey to the base metaphor of gambling: This gambling metaphor has led the industry down a road that has become both dangerous and destructive to client relationships.

Client conversations are littered with inferences of the gaming metaphor. Clients come with articles about an investment they think they want to own (tip sheet) and ask their advisor (bookie) to make the trade (book the bet). Advisors for the last decade have talked about their favorite stocks and mutual funds and their records (horses and their wins). They speak of fund managers and their experience (jockeys and their track records).

Dialogues about portfolio management include phraseology about "hedging our bets," and now, with risk clearly being of chief concern to clients, many in the industry now offer Monte Carlo simulation, which is probability analysis based on a gaming model. A dictum I often hear advisors share with clients regarding equities markets is "Don't put at risk more than you can afford to lose," which, by the way, is the very same dictum Donald Trump might share upon entering his casinos.

The metaphor that drives the business ultimately establishes the values by which the business will run and the experience that the client can expect to encounter. The gambling metaphor has demonstrated its limits in regard to both lasting values and a positive client experience. I think we can safely say that the business approach that has brought the first gazillion dollars is not the model that will bring the next gazillion dollars. Times have changed. It's time to focus on the client's *experience*.

Measuring an experience requires a different set of tools. Calculators and spreadsheets, as well as risk simulators, will come up woefully short. The tools required for measuring experience must measure emotions such as comfort, trust, and pleasantness.

Can any of us afford to build our life and practice for the future on a suspect metaphorical standard like gambling? The time has come to introduce a more promising and accurate archetype for the good of the client, the good of the advisor, and the good of the industry. The metaphor is the practice of medicine, based on one of the finest health care organizations in the world, the Mayo Clinic. The analogy for your practice is *wealth care*, designed to help clients achieve *fiscal well-being*.

If you suspect, as I do, that the wealth care metaphor is more fitting, you will then need to audit your own client experience (including language, reporting, professionalism, etc.) to see whether it reflects this picture of caring for one's clients. I favor this sort of analogy because I suspect that beyond one's personal health and family relationships, money is third in the pecking order of life.

The economics of the industry are tied to the experience of the client. No one will argue this fact. This is true at both the macro- and microlevels. I have seen this demonstrated time and again with advisors who understand the need for a new client dialogue that leads to an outstanding client experience. The average advisor has, at best, 40 percent of their average client's assets under management (AUM). They want to get 100 percent under management. Yet one must first face the reality that what got you to 40 percent *is not* the same methodology that will get you to 100 percent.

I have met scores of advisors whose clients routinely entrust *all* their assets to them and can draw but one conclusion as to why. The "why" is their focus on the client's experience and their personal focus, as an advisor, on the well-being of their client.

## How to Become a World-Class Advisor

Having lived for the past 20 years in Rochester, Minnesota, and having had the experience of seeing five (out of six) members in my household experience surgery and treatment at the Mayo Clinic, I am quite familiar with the world-class organization Drs. William and Charles Mayo founded.

The most remarkable fact to me is the fact that this organization has maintained its premier status in health care many decades after the deaths of these two brilliant visionaries. World-class organizations are not the result of simply being smart or staying busy; world-class organizations are the result of a purposefully maintained focus on core values that always revolve around the well-being of the client. A century ago, the Mayo brothers established three core values that pulsate through every client interaction in every department of the Mayo Clinic today: competence, caring, and integrity.

Contrast this ethos with that of the average health maintenance organization (HMO) whose "values," by virtue of demonstration, have proven to be largely material in nature. "See as many patients as possible. Give as little as you have to. Squeeze the most income out of every hour of patient contact." While many HMOs have prostituted the term *patient care* to the point that it feels like an assembly line for the infirm, the Mayo Clinic thrives because its values are anchored in human decency, and it puts the well-being and comfort of its clients above all other considerations.

Which model (Mayo or the average HMO) do you suppose comes to mind when the investor is asked to comment on the financial services industry? I suppose it would depend on the "experience" they have had with their own advisor.

Just how effective can this ethos-driven, client-focused approach to wealth care cause you or your firm to become? To answer, allow me to testify as to how effective and reputable this approach has helped the Mayo Clinic to become.

While conducting training programs in different parts of the country, I often ask people in the audience how many of them have personally (or know someone who has) been to the Mayo Clinic. Once in a small group with 30 advisors in Philadelphia, 27 hands went up. I then asked, "How is it with over 1,000 miles between us and with thousands of other clinics to choose from that 90 percent of you have been to my town for medical care? How could this be possible? Do you suppose it has something to do with the experience with which the Mayo Clinic provides the patient? Do you suppose it is because of the core values that every person at Mayo is taught to reflect in every patient interaction?"

I then asked for someone in this audience who had personally visited to share their impressions. A woman raised her hand. I asked, "What was your experience like?"

"Unbelievable. I have never experienced anything like it!" she began, and went on to testify of an experience that illustrated both the competence and the caring she received in equal doses.

I then asked this audience of advisors, "If I were to interview one of your clients at random and ask them what their experience with you was like, would they begin with, 'Unbelievable. I have never experienced anything like it!?'"

I do know of advisors and planners whose clients do testify this way. If I could give you their phone numbers so you could inquire yourself as to how what they do is different from what you do, you would probably find out that they have built a world-class business on the same set of values as the Mayo Clinic: competence, caring, and integrity. World-class businesses are the product of world-class values, which are always concerned with rewarding and enriching the client through their experience. And, irony of ironies, it also turns out that those same advisors are also top performers financially—doing the right thing pays off morally and monetarily.

## Edward Advisor, MD (Money Doctor)

> *I will heal them and reveal to them abundance of prosperity and security.*
>
> —Jeremiah 33:6

What clients need today is health and well-being in their financial lives. The more money Americans make, the less they sleep. The more money many people make, the more it increases their levels of stress. People typically come to advisors because there is "pain" somewhere in their financial life or there is fear of future "illness";

they need a fiscal checkup. They need and want diagnosis. Too often, however, the "MD" they come to visit has a pill to sell, no matter what ails them.

I developed the WealthCare Checkup™ (see Figure 7.1) in the hopes that some practitioners would begin a more holistic dialogue with their clients regarding the impact of both wealth accumulation and management in their lives. Money and its measures (returns, losses, gains, etc.) do not stand in a quantitative vacuum but impact every aspect of our present and future lives in some way, shape, or form. This checkup examines the following areas of one's financial life:

- Financial Sensory System (awareness of financial issues)
- Financial Respiratory System (cash flow management)
- Financial Immune System (risk management)
- Financial Cardio System (relationships that are affected by money)
- Financial Lifestyle

Positioning your practice in the wealth care paradigm will require a conversation akin to this to demonstrate that you "get it," with the "it" being the link between one's wealth and one's well-being.

Imagine the meaningful and well-rounded dialogue you could engage in with your clients and that could be launched from an assessment such as this. Yes, clients need to bring all their assets to the table to get a realistic view of how they are doing, but experience shows that they will not do so without a compelling dialogue that provokes such disclosure.

## The Practitioner's Oath

The first dictum of all advisor/client relationships could rightly be borrowed from the Hippocratic Oath: *first do no harm.*

How long can a physician expect to thrive if he or she approaches every patient appointment with the thought, "I wonder what I can sell to or gather from this patient"? It might be worth noting that physicians were not as highly regarded as professionals in our society until they stopped being paid for the drugs they recommended. Read what you will into that analogy.

A few years ago, the *Harvard Business Review* published an article, "Cluing in Customers," by Leonard L. Berry and Neeli Bendapudi,

# FINANCIAL DIAGNOSIS
## Self-Assessment

### PURPOSE

Diagnosis is essential to understanding and improving your relationship with money. The Financial Diagnosis Self-Assessment and Workbook are designed to help you increase personal awareness of the many aspects of your financial well-being.

### DIRECTIONS

For each of the 40 statements, quickly choose the response that best reflects your feelings or behavior. Your first reaction is what you should record. Write the number of your selection in the right-hand column. When you have completed all 40 statements, add the numbers in each section and record the subtotal in the place provided. On the last page, add the subtotal for your Wealth Care Total.

**Figure 7.1 WealthCare Checkup™**

**SECTION 1    FINANCIAL SENSORY SYSTEM                    NUMBER**

**1.** *My financial life is a source of frustration and inner conflict.*
   **1.** Always agree    **2.**    **3.** Halfway agree    **4.**    **5.** Never agree

**2.** *Financial matters are of no interest to me.*
   **1.** Always agree    **2.**    **3.** Halfway agree    **4.**    **5.** Never agree

**3.** *I have identified specific financial goals.*
   **1.** Not at all like me    **2.**    **3.** Halfway like me    **4.**    **5.** Exactly like me

**4.** *I have a good understanding of the important financial issues that need to be addressed at this stage of my life.*
   **1.** Not at all like me    **2.**    **3.** Halfway like me    **4.**    **5.** Exactly like me

**5.** *I will consider an investment only when I'm guaranteed not to lose any money.*
   **1.** Exactly like me    **2.**    **3.** Halfway like me    **4.**    **5.** Not at all like me

**6.** *I am attracted to get rich quick tips and ideas.*
   **1.** Exactly like me    **2.**    **3.** Halfway like me    **4.**    **5.** Not at all like me

**7.** *I feel that at this point in my life,*
   **1.** I am way behind where I expected to be financially
   **2.** I am somewhat behind where I expected to be financially
   **3.** I am about where I expected to be financially
   **4.** I am ahead of where I expected to be financially
   **5.** I am way ahead of where I expected to be financially

**8.** *I worry about not having enough money in later life.*
   **1.** Exactly like me    **2.**    **3.** Halfway like me    **4.**    **5.** Not at all like me

                                        **SECTION 1    Subtotal**

**SECTION 2    FINANCIAL RESPIRATORY SYSTEM                NUMBER**

**9.** *My financial records are well-organized.*
   **1.** Not at all like me    **2.**    **3.** Halfway like me    **4.**    **5.** Exactly like me

**10.** *I have gotten the help I need to assess my financial picture.*
   **1.** Not at all like me    **2.**    **3.** Halfway like me    **4.**    **5.** Exactly like me

**11.** *The way I manage money is consistent with my priorities in life.*
   **1.** Always agree    **2.**    **3.** Halfway agree    **4.**    **5.** Never agree

**12.** *This is how long I estimate it will take before I will be able to live the life I want:*
   **1.** I have no idea    **2.** Over 10 years    **3.** 6-10 years    **4.** 1-5 years    **5.** I'm there now

**13.** *In regard to my saving habits,*
   **1.** I overspend and have too much debt to save    **3.** I save when I can
   **2.** I spend what I earn and there is none        **4.** I save regularly, but not enough
      left over to save                                **5.** I save regularly, and adequately to meet my goals

**14.** *I frequently make purchases spontaneously.*
   **1.** Exactly like me    **2.**    **3.** Halfway like me    **4.**    **5.** Not at all like me

**15.** *I am taking full advantage of my tax advantaged retirement plan opportunities such as IRA, 401(k) s, deferred compensation, etc.*
   **1.** Not at all like me    **2.**    **3.** Halfway like me    **4.**    **5.** Exactly like me

**16.** *I check my progress towards meeting my financial goals on a regular basis.*
   **1.** Not at all like me    **2.**    **3.** Halfway like me    **4.**    **5.** Exactly like me

                                        **SECTION 2    Subtotal**

**Figure 7.1**   *(continued)*

**SECTION 3** — **FINANCIAL IMMUNE SYSTEM** — **NUMBER**

**17.** *I am well protected against major financial loss caused by extended illness, disability, long-term care, or downturn in the stock market.*
1. Not at all like me    2.    3. Halfway like me    4.    5. Exactly like me

**18.** *If I were to miss a month's pay, I would experience serious financial problems.*
1. Exactly like me    2.    3. Halfway like me    4.    5. Not at all like me

**19.** *I have skills, knowledge, and/or talents that are transferable and in demand in the job market.*
1. Not at all like me    2.    3. Halfway like me    4.    5. Exactly like me

**20.** *In the past, I have been creative in finding ways to earn extra income when I have needed or wanted it.*
1. Not at all like me    2.    3. Halfway like me    4.    5. Exactly like me

**21.** *I feel defeated when I think about my financial future.*
1. Always agree    2.    3. Halfway agree    4.    5. Never agree

**22.** *If I were to lose half of my income, I could successfully navigate the transition.*
1. Not at all like me    2.    3. Halfway like me    4.    5. Exactly like me

**23.** *I feel I have the skills and knowledge needed to build financial security.*
1. Not at all like me    2.    3. Halfway like me    4.    5. Exactly like me

**24.** *I'm easily confused or intimidated by financial terminology or jargon.*
1. Always agree    2.    3. Halfway agree    4.    5. Never agree

**SECTION 3**    Subtotal

**SECTION 4** — **FINANCIAL CARDIO SYSTEM** — **NUMBER**

**25.** *Financial issues cause a lot of tension in a relationship that is important to me.*
1. Always agree    2.    3. Halfway agree    4.    5. Never agree

**26.** *I experience a lot of frustration when discussing financial matters with certain family members.*
1. Always agree    2.    3. Halfway agree    4.    5. Never agree

**27.** *I am concerned about the impact of meeting the costs of higher education.*
1. Exactly like me    2.    3. Halfway like me    4.    5. Not at all like me

**28.** *I often feel squeezed between the competing financial needs and wants of family members (spouse/partner, children, parents, etc.).*
1. Always agree    2.    3. Halfway agree    4.    5. Never agree

**29.** *I feel comfortable talking with financial professionals (i.e., accountants, bankers, investment representatives, etc.) about my financial matters.*
1. Never agree    2.    3. Halfway agree    4.    5. Always agree

**30.** *I feel confident in my ability to evaluate the accuracy and appropriateness of the financial advice I receive.*
1. Not at all like me    2.    3. Halfway like me    4.    5. Exactly like me

**31.** *A major goal for my money is helping others and/or supporting causes.*
1. Not at all like me    2.    3. Halfway like me    4.    5. Exactly like me

**32.** *Charitable giving is currently an essential element of my financial plan.*
1. Not at all like me    2.    3. Halfway like me    4.    5. Exactly like me

**SECTION 4**    Subtotal

**Figure 7.1** *(continued)*

| SECTION 5 | FINANCIAL LIFESTYLE | NUMBER |
|---|---|---|

**33.** *If I could, I would change the kind of work I do.*
1. Always agree　　2.　　3. Halfway agree　　4.　　5. Never agree

**34.** *I engage in paid or unpaid "work" that gives my life a sense of purpose.*
1. Never agree　　2.　　3. Halfway agree　　4.　　5. Always agree

**35.** *I have a difficult time clarifying what is most important to me.*
1. Exactly like me　　2.　　3. Halfway like me　　4.　　5. Not at all like me

**36.** *I've spent a lot of money trying to find happiness.*
1. Exactly like me　　2.　　3. Halfway like me　　4.　　5. Not at all like me

**37.** *I feel I do not spend adequate time with the people I love.*
1. Always agree　　2.　　3. Halfway agree　　4.　　5. Never agree

**38.** *I feel like my life revolves around making money.*
1. Always agree　　2.　　3. Halfway agree　　4.　　5. Never agree

**39.** *I am motivated to take charge of my financial life.*
1. Never agree　　2.　　3. Halfway agree　　4.　　5. Always agree

**40.** *I am committed to discovering my emotional roadblocks to achieving financial well-being.*
1. Not at all like me　　2.　　3. Halfway like me　　4.　　5. Exactly like me

**SECTION 5**　Subtotal

*In each of the five sections, add the numbers to determine subtotal scores. The maximum subtotal for each section is 40.*

*Next, enter the subtotal in the grid below and add together for your Wealth Care Total. The maximum Wealth Care Total is 200.*

**Section 1 Subtotal**

**Section 2 Subtotal**

**Section 3 Subtotal**

**Section 4 Subtotal**

**Section 5 Subtotal**

**WealthCare Total**

Financial *life* Planning Institute
www.financialifeplanning.com

in which the authors studied the success of the Mayo Clinic at repeatedly offering patients a superior experience with "Evidence Management." Evidence Management, according to the writers, is an organized, explicit approach to presenting customers with coherent, honest evidence of your abilities. "Evidence Management," they wrote, "is a lot like advertising, except that it turns a company into a living, breathing advertisement of itself."

This also will become the new focus of conducting the business of financial advice, where advertising imprints will no longer be primarily relied upon to sway customer opinion, but where representatives of the best companies will become "living, breathing advertisements" of the highest professional standards and values.

When we do not feel well or are seeking a doctor or medical clinic, we all instinctively turn into top-rate detectives. Why? Because something precious and irreplaceable is at stake: our physical well-being. We conduct scrutinizing inspections of doctors and clinics for evidence of competence, caring, and integrity. If we fail to see evidence of any of these three and we have a choice, we move on.

Since the market downturn, widespread reports of corruption, and 9/11, Americans are now applying the identical detective work to their choice of financial advisor because something precious and irreplaceable is at stake: their *fiscal* well-being. Companies can no longer afford to leave the evidence that clients view to chance. Every interaction, from the reception desk to the back office, must demonstrate competence, caring, and integrity. Clients are going to a place where they will be cared for, where people are educated and live up to their titles, and where they are treated to unbending standards of integrity.

Welcome to the world of WealthCare, where the practitioner's primary concern is not selling drugs but caring for patients.

## ReSOULution

Lead with integrity, follow with caring, and execute with competence. All three are attractive to us as human beings, but finding all three in one source is in short supply. Determine to be just such a source. Every human being rests in the knowledge that they are being dealt with squarely, that they are cared about as people, and that their affairs are being managed with excellence. It is the business definition of the Golden Rule.

# CHAPTER 8

# The New Frontier

## GETTING TO THE RIGHT SIDE OF THE ADVISORY BUSINESS

*Future products will have to appeal to our hearts, not to our heads.*
*Now is the time to add emotional value to products and services.*
— Rolf Jensen, *Dream Society*

Joe, a senior executive in the financial services industry with over 30 years experience, told me that he had recently had a very sophisticated financial plan developed. When the time came for the planner to present the plan, Joe said, "This thing is as thick as a mid-size city phone book and makes absolutely no sense to me. It was a confusing and confounding pile of paper. I left thinking, 'What in the world does that have to do with what I want out of life and my money?' This guy was great with processes; he just didn't have a clue about me. If I've been in this industry for 33 years and can't comprehend this, what in the world is it like for the average Joe?"

Is there anything truly unique or compelling in telling your clients that you are good at fund selection, asset allocation, probability analysis, financial planning, or any other technical function that has become ubiquitous in the financial landscape? Are we in danger of exhausting the technical and tactical well and becoming extremely vulnerable to the forces of commoditization? (Commoditization: the daunting and obdurate force that is attended by the two hooded horsemen of the advisory apocalypse—expanded competition and shrinking margins.)

The prominent lesson I'm learning regarding today's advisory/ planning marketplace is that most of the existing value propositions are based in the left side of the brain. Multiplying and dividing, analyzing and allocating, selecting and projecting are all left-brain functions and processes that, while being valuable, are easily duplicated and consequently commoditized. These functions are the last remnants of a scientific age and ideology that, in my opinion, are now on life support. How much more value is left in measuring, calculating, projecting, and scrutinizing when everyone purports to do it and we have standardized tools for doing it? The present age calls for us to trade in our microscopes for a magnetic resonance imaging (MRI) machine that will help us see into the inside of the matter that which cannot be observed (or measured) on the surface.

An example is the certified financial planning (CFP) inculcation that intimates that the heightened ability to manage, manipulate, and project numbers, and to produce sophisticated financial plans will sustain the business. Yet you could be the greatest tactician in the world and still be completely clueless as to how to connect with a prospect or client.

The new frontier in financial services in on the inside of the matter. The interior concerns, hopes, stories, lessons, experiences, regrets, and dictates attached to each client's money is the true driving force for where they will park that money and whom they will hand the keys to.

## Right Turn Ahead

The new frontier for building your business is in mastering those functions that cannot become a commodity; those functions and competencies are based in the right side of your brain. These are the *intuitive* functions: establishing context for the work you will do; discovering the basis for their hopes and fears; conceptualizing, strategizing, sensing, and connecting with key emotional drivers. Every astute student of financial advice and planning acknowledges that this business boils down to helping clients formulate and actualize their dreams. *It's about using money to making the uttermost of their innermost.*

*Take a look at your conventional overstuffed garage. Paradoxically,*
*affluence has not led to fulfillment. Of course, the search for*
*meaning takes place in the right brain.*
                                    —Daniel H. Pink, *Wired* magazine

This is where the great upside exists: Learning to master your intuitive skill sets. Table 8.1 contrasts the left- and right-side functions. You may have already observed that every function listed in the left side is up against both expanding competition and contracting margins and fees.

The fact is that the left brain is attempting to analyze, and the right brain is attempting to synthesize. While the left brain attempts to gather and organize content, the right brain seeks to discover the living context for all this information. While the left side is digging for details and facts, the right side seeks the *emotional information* by gathering stories and formulating the big picture.

The left side is trying to get itself around the means (the raw material substance; what it is and how it will be used) and the right

**Table 8.1   Getting It Right: Business Intelligence**

|  | Left-Brain Information | Right-Brain Intuition |
|---|---|---|
| **Focuses on** | Detail | Big picture |
|  | Information | Emotions |
|  | Quantitative | Qualitative |
|  | Facts | Stories |
|  | Content | Context |
|  | Rationale | Relational |
|  | Means | Meaning |
| **Processes by** | Investigating | Sensing |
|  | Reading the lines | Reading between the lines |
|  | Calculating/organizing | Integrating |
|  | Analyzing | Synthesizing |
|  | Justifying | Bridging |
|  | Calculating means | Deciphering meaning |
| **Outputs** | Information | Narrative |
|  | Mathematics | Metaphors |
|  | Debates | Dialogues |
|  | Story of numbers | Number of stories |
|  | Technical insight | Strategic insight |

side is trying to wrap itself around what this all means (the meaning and purpose of all this "stuff").

There is curiosity present in both sides of the brain, although the left side is concerned with that which can be quantified and measured, and the right side is curious about the qualitative—the emotional story read between the lines that is better weighed that measured. The end product that benefits the client in the utilization of full-brain advice is a superior form of *strategic insight.*

Strategic insight that hits the bull's-eye with a client's deepest wishes and goals is hardly possible without an understanding of *who* a client is that is as thorough as *what* a client has and *where* they have it stored.

Who the client is, why they want what they want, who they will trust and why they will trust them, what emotions are attached to the assets they have gathered, and how they are to be distributed are the *right side* of this business—a frontier on the inside of the client and the potential that exists inside the advisor that we have hardly begun to recognize or explore. That will all change in the years ahead.

## Turning the Inside Out

The financial services industry is concerned with the external issues of money by definition but has stumbled in recent years into the internal realities that surround the external realm. This had led to practitioners' scrambling to both understand and give the impression of understanding around topics like goal setting, life planning, behavioral finance, and financial coaching, which are all euphemistic of *internal finance.*

I suspect that the successful advisors of the near future will be those who both understand these internal aspects and have successfully integrated them into their practices, seamlessly, with the external mechanics of money.

The evolution of the industry from the description of *broker* (a term implying competence with the external aspects of money manipulation) to the description of *advisor* (a term implying cogency and understanding) in and of itself has raised the premium on finding and training individuals who can manage both the internal and external aspects of the advisor/client/money triangular relationship. The very term *advisor* implies something internal in nature: experience, insight, wisdom, and understanding of matters.

The advisory skill set is a quantum leap from a strictly sales-oriented skill set.

The fact that the external aspects of this business have been largely commoditized has provided plenty of incentive for individuals and institutions looking to remain competitive to search into the realm of the internal for value-added propositions in their client relationships. Once you enter the internal aspects of learning surrounding money, you find yourself in a candy store of possibilities in that the skills and competencies you learn do not burn with the short fuse of standardization and commoditization.

There is plenty of profit potential ahead in exploring the wisdom, insight, understanding, fears, psychic realities, motivations, and potentialities of today's client, but also in exploring the fact that these things are all wrapped up in the very substance itself. No one with an ounce of understanding around the topic of money will deny the unique energy (psychic, spiritual, and emotional) that emanates from money and the money/trust conversation.

## Seeking Brain-Damaged Clients

Recently, I heard Michael Mauboussin, author of *More than You Know: Finding Financial Wisdom in Unconventional Places,* a fascinatingly easy read replete with profound wisdom on investment issues from realms outside of institutional investments. He shared an anecdote about a study that was conducted between "normal" people and those where the emotional seat was damaged; that is, they did not emote as regular folks do over common circumstances. The experiment went as follows: Twenty rounds of a gamble were conducted. It was a coin flip where, if they won, they received $1.25, and if they lost, they lost $1.00.

In a game like this, "investment rationale" informs you that you will flip the coin into infinity because the odds are stacked in your favor. The obvious odds of a coin flip, over time, are 50 percent. If you flipped the coin 100 times and called heads every single time and it came out heads only 45 times you would still be ahead. So what happened in the experiment?

When "normal" people lost a round or two or a few in a row, they became risk averse and stopped taking this proper and rational risk; those with damage in the emotional side of the brain forged ahead knowing that, over time, the flip would tip their way.

The simple lesson here is that "emotional detachment" from losses serves one in the investment realm. But this is easier preached than practiced. One of the primary lessons that has been gleaned from studies in behavioral finance is that we suffer losses twice as much as we enjoy gains. *Pain trumps gain* is all you need to remember the next time you see a client ready to run for the hills over a dip in the market after you have, maybe even recently, helped them achieve respectable gains in the same market environment.

Every advisor worth their salt knows that, after a difficult period in the market, we need to "stay in the game" as equities are then discounted and opportunity is ripe. But every advisor also knows what an uphill emotional battle this can be to convince a client of "logic" when emotion has them by the throat.

## Financial Pitfalls

As an individual who believes that the greatest progress we can make in the money realm is in understanding the emotional/psychological/spiritual drivers and influences that control the material, I'm thrilled to see the strides that have been made by Daniel Kahneman and others in the field of behavioral finance. Doesn't this intellectual leap tell us something of the new frontier? My disappointment is in the inability of retail planners to address these all-too-pertinent facts of finance with their clients.

I suspect that the blame does not necessarily lie with the retail planner and advisor. I think a part of the problem is the academic language that these behavioral revelations are couched in. It is not everyday language to use terms like *framing, confirmation trap,* and *dissonance,* but these issues affect your business in a profound way every single day.

What is needed, and what I suspect we will see very soon, is some translation work that puts these findings into everyday language and into easily understood illustrations and analogies. Once the insights become more accessible, I suspect we will see more advisors engage their clients in these discussions.

One caveat: it takes a certain degree of courage and tact to confront clients with issues of emotion trumping reason. (I suspect the answer lies in speaking in global terms, "We all struggle with . . ."). No one wants to feel stupid, and the fact remains that we all make irrational decisions around money for very emotional reasons.

This, too, is a piece of the puzzle that must be solved to remedy the disconnect between decisive emotion and investment results.

I would challenge you to begin thinking about how you will translate some of the pertinent discoveries of behavioral finance into your client conversations. For example, how will you translate and converse on:

**Overconfidence:** Where your clients' outcome range is too narrow and they have unrealistic expectations in getting those results.

**Anchoring:** Where clients tend to anchor on past events or trends and read far too much into past patterns.

**Framing effects:** Where the temptation is strong to sell winners and hold losers because we can then frame those decisions to make us look smart.

**Confirmation trap:** Where we seek only confirming information and dismiss or discount disconfirming information, again because we do not want to look bad (dissonance) and where the famous last words are, "Mistakes were made but not by me."

Ego is a problem. This seems obvious. Ego is an internal issue, and it cannot be ignored in the advisory realm.

## Nerves that Steal

Regret, denial, anxiety, greed: these terms don't exactly sound like quantifiable issues, do they? However, we know that they are the drivers of quantifiable wealth and a cornerstone of the next frontier in understanding how to manage client expectations and behaviors.

In his book *Your Money and Your Brain*, Jason Zweig introduces us to the term *neuroeconomics,* a term that amalgamates economics, psychology, and neuroscience and attempts to explain why the brain is a battleground between reason and emotion when it comes to money. Some important concepts are raised in this field that every financial advisor would do well to contemplate and develop client dialogues around. Here are a few of my favorites:

**The Inner Con Man:** Zweig states that every client and every advisor has one; the inner con man is always telling you lies about why things worked and why they didn't.

**Risk Tolerance Is Intellectual Fraud:** this is something I have been railing against in financial services industry for the last decade. It is absurd to think clients can realistically explain or quantify their risk tolerance. Risk tolerance surveys are like asking someone, "In the case of an earthquake, what would you do?," to which your client replies, "I would do my best to save everyone who was trapped first." Sure, you would. Nobody knows what they would do until they are faced with the circumstance. This was proven in the bear market of 2001–2002, where suddenly everyone was "conservative" in their approach, especially those whose risk tolerance questionnaires indicated "aggressive."

**The More You Know, the Worse You Do:** Here's a lesson that was first learned on the race track. When handicappers are given more information about horses, their confidence level rises but not in proportion to their success level. Handicappers with 15 bits of information were much more confident in their picks than those with only five pieces, even though their results didn't reflect this confidence. (Can you see yourself in this analogy?)

**Managing Expectations Is Worth More than Managing Assets:** Anticipation trumps realization for losses and gains. The actual loss is not as bad as a client thought and the actual gains were not as rewarding as they hoped. The emotional net/net of expectations carrying more weight than realizations is that it only succeeds in discouraging necessary risk.

**The Importance of Rules, Procedures, and Policies:** At the end of the day the best method discovered for keeping emotions in the penalty box is to have hard-and-fast rules and procedures in place that you and your clients' emotions must defer to when tempted to engage in whimsical behavior. If we say we don't want more than 10 percent concentration in one stock and we have a winner that is shooting to the moon, we must sell some of it because it threatens our policy on concentration. If we say we will buy only equities that we are comfortable holding for at least three years, we have to stay away from flip-flopping. We must define (ahead of time) our policy regarding emotional responses to market's ups and downs. By the way, if you are trying to develop long-term mind-sets and relationships, why do you have a monitor with a stock ticker in your office?

I firmly believe that one answer to the dangers of "emotionomic" issues facing your clients and your practice is in expanding the investment policy statement toward defining, for every client, a sound *fiscalosophy* because, if we have learned anything from these emerging fields and from our experience, it is that *how you think about your money is as important as how you manage it.*

## Not Like Politics

Recently, a successful advisor came to me after I delivered a speech on the intuitive side of this business and remarked, "All the things you were talking about—reading between the lines, getting the client's story, figuring out the meaning of their money and what emotions are associated with it—have always come very naturally to me. I just struggle with doing all that versus all the technical and tactical processes (which I also do quite well with) that my company tells me are what are most important and that we advertise as our chief value."

"You don't have a problem," I told him. "You have a gift. The word you need to purge from your description is *versus*. This is not an either/or proposition, right brain versus left, intuitive versus intellectual—these functions are designed as the perfect complement. This is not like politics, where the left and right are at odds with one another. In your brain they are the ultimate allies seeking to blend the emotional and factual into one synthetic solution."

I also brought to the attention of this advisor that part of the problem is that in the educational process, both academically and in corporate inculcation, we were always taught to place a premium on left brain skills. IQ is measured this way; scholarships and promotions are often given on this basis.

Things are beginning to change. We're rapidly approaching the law of diminishing returns on number crunching, analytical, and micromanagement functions at the retail level. Today's market is calling for more. They are seeking insight, experience, interpretation, and, ultimately, wisdom. How do we begin to prepare for such a marketplace? These functions are not done in the left-side computer and the machines that mimic it; they are done in the blender that mixes, chops, and purees all the elements at play and shows us what we have.

It will also become important to understand the organic order in which these functions need to operate. The big-picture, contextual work of the right brain needs to precede the small-picture, detail work of the left. We need to weigh a client's emotional comfort level with our recommendations before we implement those ideas. We need to figure out the objectives for the money before we decide where to direct that money.

I continually see advisors who have the (right) stuff to offer diminishing their value proposition to reflect commoditized services (that are measured by numbers) such as asset management, financial planning, probability analysis, and other quantifiable and easily competed against functions. I think that this is because even though they possess the intuitive functions, they do not know how to sell the "right" stuff.

Once the skilled, intuitive advisor learns how to sell the stuff and services of right-brain origin, no one can compete with him nor turn his value proposition of insight into a commodity, because the right-side value proposition is about how well I know you, how tuned in I am to your situation, how much I care about you reaching your potential and making your life count, and how well I pay attention on an ongoing basis. What price will the consumer pay for this value proposition? There is abundantly more economic upside in the "right-side proposition than there is in the expanding competition/ shrinking margin left-side proposition.

There is only one way out of the hell of comparative numbers driving your life and business: plant your value proposition squarely in the right side of your client's brain.

I would much more prefer to deal with numbers in the context of matters that are weighed than to deal only with things measured— percentages, returns, rates, analyses, and probabilities. The very words sedate me. They are a dime a dozen in today's marketplace. They are too easy to calculate, and all one needs is a calculator.

But the other matters, the things that are weighed, by conscience, intuition, spirit, and imagination, are implied, inferred, read between the lines, and intuitively discerned. The very words excite every cell of being and intelligence, to say nothing of the financial planning process, which they bring to life, literally. Measuring is what we do with the life of matter, but weighing is reserved for matters of life. It's time to start pointing this industry in the right direction.

## ReSOULution

Realize that your skill sets around the mechanics of money should be secondary to your understanding of the client and their intentions for that money. Build a higher standard for discovery of whom it is we are serving and how we can best serve them. Build your business value proposition, first and foremost, around right-brain competencies.

# PART II

# LIFE RESOULUTIONS

Money answers all" or "Money answers nothing"—which is it? Neither, actually. Money improperly utilized answers little, and money properly utilized answers much in our lives. But it can never answer everything; it simply does not have that power. Many in our society need to ponder the question asked by an ancient prophet who asked, "Why spend money on what is not bread, and your labor on what does not satisfy? Listen, listen to me, and eat what is good and your soul will delight in the richest of fare" (Isaiah 55:2).

I'm reminded of the story I heard of the multimillionaire standing on his roof making a call during the Katrina crisis and saying, "The water is up to my roof, I have one drink of water left, and my cell phone battery is running out. I'm worth five million dollars—what good is it now?" In this case not much good, but in most cases it can do an awful lot of good when put in proper perspective and utilized in a way that delivers greater satisfaction and gratification with life in general.

# CHAPTER 9

# Permanent Reference Points

## HOW THE FINANCIAL BLUEPRINT IS FORMED

*We are so closely identified with our dollars. Money represents us:
our toil, our time, and our talent. The real value of any currency
lies in its symbolism. It stands for the brawn and brains of those
who earned it. Money is concentrated personality, or personality
in coin. Our picture may not be on any dollar bill but our person
certainly is in it.*

—Leslie B. Flynn

Grandma, do you think there's a sugar shortage soon?" Jack
asked as he and his wife and kids watched her stuff a dozen packets
or so from the restaurant table into her purse. Next in were two
dinner rolls, butter packets (wrapped in spare napkins), and a fist-
ful of the small plastic half-and-half containers.

"Honey, you just never know," she said, repeating a refrain that
his father, Jack, and now his children had been hearing for years.
Though Grandma's cupboards were full and her bank account plenti-
ful, she lived emotionally and perpetually on the very edge of poverty
and extinction. The scarce meats and rare treats of her childhood
days (one Christmas she got an orange, nothing more) in the Great
Depression were as near to her consciousness as Jack's son's unfin-
ished plate of chicken and rice upon which her gaze was transfixed.

"Maybe we should get a take-home package for that," she offered, touching the chicken plate.

"You mean a doggy bag, Great-grandma?" one of the grandchildren asked.

"No, honey, that's still people food."

Grandma's childhood experience had left indelible marks on her values, emotions, and habits. The Great Depression was a permanent reference point in Grandma's approach to material goods and money. Living for 60 years beyond that time with three hot meals a day couldn't change it. Living in a lovely home with a full pantry couldn't change it. Having a bank account with over $800,000 and living off the interest couldn't change it, either. Such experiences have a great power over our thinking and create inner realities that will guide us for the rest of our lives. Jack's grandmother's experience had become a permanent reference point.

## A Blueprint for Success

Psychological science has discovered that emotional patterns are formed very early in our lives, and emotional patterns regarding money are no different. Specific messages delivered in visceral tones and memorable experiences involving the transfer (or lack thereof) of money are tattooed in the memory bank. Consequently, these memories and messages, which author Rick Kahler refers to as *moneyscripts*, form a blueprint that guides our financial behavior for the rest of our lives.

Later in this book, I will offer a dialogue for discovering the meaningful and formative events in your client's history (Chapter 15). For this discussion on permanent reference points, I offer two questions that can help you discover experiences that are largely responsible for casting your financial mold:

- What was money like growing up?
- How do you think your family experiences with money have impacted your approach to money and investing today?

I have conducted this conversation numerous times, and it seems that the greatest good that results from the inquiry is that it allows the person being questioned to self-discover a connection that he may not have been aware of between his early years and present attitude and approach to money. You will hear stories and statements that reveal much about defining experiences:

"Looking back, we didn't have that much but it never felt like we were poor. . . ."

"It seemed that Dad and Mom worked hard just to stay above water and taught us all to look for bargains and to fix things rather than replace them. I'm still like that today. There are many things I could afford to replace with something new, but I get more pleasure by extending the life of the thing I already own."

"When I was a teen, our house burned down and we lost everything. As much as we missed certain things, we all realized how little the 'stuff' meant in light of the fact that all of us escaped with our lives."

"My dad had a business partner who made very bad decisions without my father's knowledge and he ended up having to declare bankruptcy as a result, even though he had never missed a payment in his life."

"It seemed like whenever I wanted something growing up, I got it. When I was on my own I got accustomed to this and was brought under the sway of credit cards and experienced a lot of stress as a result. I'm trying to teach my kids to earn what they get on their own and to think for a while about how badly they want the thing they think they want."

"There were certain things Mom wanted for the house that we couldn't afford with a large family and Dad's meager salary, so Mom started her own business and did quite well. Her example convinced me of the unlimited possibilities of being an entrepreneur and, I'm sure, is largely responsible for the fact that I'm a business owner today."

"My parents were wonderful, hardworking people who never allowed themselves to enjoy the fruits of their labors. I think they were afraid of being old and poor someday. We never took vacations (which frustrated me) and never did fun or spontaneous things because 'they cost too much.' I've gone the other way with my family, maybe even to a fault, but I don't care. We go on a lot of trips; do spontaneous, crazy things that cost money; and create memories every chance we get."

The stories and accompanying scripts are endless. Every client has his or her own stories and morals of those stories. Just as infinite are the implications for you, the advisor of wealth, in managing your relationship with these individuals. I find little disagreement with the idea that, as an advisor, you are better off knowing these formative experiences and blueprinting patterns than not knowing them.

Buried in these financial biographies are expectations, guideposts, myths, and origins of financial thought that you will run into sooner or later in the form of client behavior. Having a reference point for that behavior can make all the difference in the world.

## Swimming in the Financial Gene Pool

My wife has a little reference point phrase she reserves for use with me when I mirror my father's propensity for being overly thrifty ("tight" is what she might call it). The phrase she uses to jolt me into present economic realities: "*You can afford dry cleaning now.*"

The fact is that for years I didn't believe I could and I couldn't understand the concept of paying 20% of the price I might have paid to purchase a garment just to clean it. I would attempt to clean it myself. I know these patterns were inculcated and indelibly printed in my psyche by my father's messages and behaviors as I grew up. Having grown up in poverty and without a father, my father had to scrap for everything he had and had no room for "rich folks'" luxuries. He supported a family of seven on a very modest salary and never missed an opportunity to exercise frugality bordering on obsessive parsimony. The nut—in this case, me—did not fall far from the tree. My wife, recognizing the parsimonious pinch of the eyes, reminds me that a little expenditure now and then isn't going to lead us to the poor house.

All our brains are wired emotionally on the topic of money by similar messages, scripts, models of behavior, and defining experiences. We have reasons for behaving as we do with money that often fall to the subconscious level but direct our behaviors nonetheless. Rick Kahler, in his book, *Conscious Finance,* with coauthor Kathleen Fox, asserts that people can make much progress through dialogue by moving these emotionally subconscious drivers to a more recognized conscious level. Such a focus on subconscious motivation can easily lead to a psychotherapeutic approach far outside of the purview of financial advice, which is why some advisors are now referring clients they deem to be "stuck" on money issues to psychologists specializing in money issues.

I am not a proponent of teaching financial advisors psychoanalytical models, but instead teaching *discovery* models that help you to better understand what experiences and guideposts have shaped the attitude of the client whose money you are now managing. The understanding is worth its weight in gold to you. In the case of Great–grandmother, who takes sugar packets out of the restaurant because of her Depression-era reference point, you probably won't be able to budge her from her scarcity mind-set, but now, at the very least, you understand what motivates such an outlook.

## Recent Reference Points

In the past few years, clients have had some significant *imprinting* experiences that have already taken root within them and will continue their impact throughout their lives. The ephemeral event takes on infinite significance once planted in the garden of memory and watered with daily observation. As we discussed earlier, 9/11 introduced the vast majority of us to fear, to the importance of family, and to a sudden shifting of what is really important in our lives. The internal consequence regarding money is that we now long for a way to use our means as a path to meaning. After 9/11, money went from being about making a living to making a life. Recently, a financial planner from Chicago described this internal shift like this: "Before 9/11, I advised clients based on their assets. Now, I advise them based on their hearts."

I have met many advisors since that incident who straightforwardly inquire, "What changed for you because of 9/11?"

Something changed for all of us, individually and collectively. How do those changes impact our relationship to our money? For some, it meant saving more because of fear and uncertainty. For others, it meant spending more because of the brevity of life.

## Reference Point: The Last Market Downtown

*The darkest hour of any man's life is when he sits down to plan
how to make money without earning it.*

—Horace Greeley

Some of us can remember back when we partook of a drunken investment orgy around a golden calf until that idol came crashing down with our individual dreams and hopes amalgamated into its molten form. The stock markets had become the golden calf. Worshippers were engaged in a manic ritual of checking prices by the hour and keeping an umbilical connection to CNBC and online portfolios. Now, with the calf fallen, the same people who could not avert their eyes in the frenzy of a rising market cannot bring themselves to open their 401(k) statement lest their eyes tell them the truth.

The market downturn rattled and shook the cuckoo's nest out of the easy-money tree that had captured so many of our imaginations and assets. Many nest eggs were broken and injured as the nest fell to the ground. At the very least, we all received a much-needed wake-up call. The internal consequence is that we now realize our vulnerability to financial foolishness, greed, and unrealistic expectations. We know that smart people can and will do very foolish things when it comes to money. Hopefully, their memory will serve them well the next time they are tempted.

A retired woman in her mid-sixties who had far too much market exposure during the downturn and lost 35 percent of her assets for retirement, commented to me, "I just need to get it back to close to what it was." This emotional expectation or need to "get it back close to what it was" is setting her up for another mistake as the emotional pendulum swings from greed to fear.

Behavioral finance is an academic attempt to explain the often irrational behaviors that lure intelligent people into their grips because of their inability to "face" mistakes they have made, are making, or are about to make with their money.

One advisor told me he asks every prospective client this question, "Do you remember what went through your mind when you read your financial statements at the end of 2002? What lessons did you learn, and how have you applied them?" This was his method of understanding how this reference point had impacted their relationship to their money and money managers.

Any person who lost money in a bear market remembers the feeling and the outtakes from that experience just as a person who had to declare bankruptcy or lost a home or saw a fortune disappear would remember. These recollections are key reference points for understanding your client's parameters for whom they will trust and where they will feel safe in the future.

## Reference Point: Corporate and Industry Corruption

When a man messes with my money, he is messing with me. It is more than chicanery. It is more than selfish salesmanship. It is even more than exploitation. It is a personal insult at the deepest level because that individual or company failed to realize the price I had to pay to bring that money to the table.

The revelations of corruption in the financial sector broke what trust remained between Main Street and Wall Street. Clients were told to do things that the advisors themselves wouldn't do. In the client's mind, the numbers were used to deceive. The greatest mistake we can make is to underestimate the damage that's been done and the germ of cynicism that has taken hold. When clients look at their personal financial situations, are they aware that they could use some help? This is fairly complicated stuff, but where do they turn for help given corruption reports and our collective experiences? They don't really want to manage their own money affairs completely on their own, but no longer have a clue as to whom they can trust to help them. All eyes are now wide open for the duplicitous purveyors of "advice."

The internal need is for determining what it is going to take to rebuild that trust or if one cares to cross that bridge at all. If a person chooses to manage assets, risk, debt, tax, distribution, and estate matters on their own, then they are faced with a daunting learning curve and must decide to dedicate themselves to planning competence. This proposition will carry a measure of stress with it, and at some point that stress can outweigh the benefits of autonomous advice. They also must make an honest and aware assessment of their own ability (with time and knowledge limitations) to manage such affairs alone.

Should they choose to work with professional planners, experts, and advisors, consumers must now answer the question of how they will measure the sincerity and integrity of those people who offer financial "services."

Now is the time for the emergence of a new breed of financial planner that will rise to the top of the profession and truly put the needs of the client first in the financial planning process. These professionals recognize the wide chasm of distrust that exists in our society and are rebuilding a bridge by laying all cards on the table, removing conflicts of interest, and making the client's life the hub around which the plan revolves, as opposed to their own self-serving ideas, products, or services.

## ReSOULution

Form deep and lasting bonds with others by connecting with the touchpoints in the histories that have shaped their philosophies, values, and goals in life. Each person is a product of formative experiences that left indelible impressions upon their psyche and soul. To understand those experiences is to understand their reasons for being and reasons for behaving as they do.

# 10

# How We Measure Money

*Money is best measured not by a story of numbers but by a number of stories.*

—Mitch Anthony

I knew the phone call from my mother was going to be laborious when she opened with, "I don't think Grandpa would be too proud."

"What's this about, Mom?" I asked.

"It's been one year and one week since Daddy died," she said, "and I feel so bad about what I've done with the money."

"What's happened with the money, Mom?" I inquired.

"Well, first of all, I invested a big chunk of it with a friend," she placed the word *friend* in noticeable tonal, "and it's lost a lot of its value and now my 'friend' no longer returns my phone calls. When I finally did get through to someone in his office, they informed me that if I were to move the money I would be penalized on top of my already substantial losses."

"How much money have you lost, Mom?" I asked, fearing the answer I would receive. Her answer forever changed how I would view money. It was an epiphany on why there is such a wide chasm of understanding and trust between advisor and client in the financial services industry. Her answer informed me that I knew nothing about how money is measured.

"I have lost five years of Daddy's hard work." She could barely choke out the words and began to weep.

Her father, my grandfather, Sylvester Aloyicious Babinski, was a second-generation Polish immigrant farmer in the state of "Nort" Dakota (Sylvester's pronunciation). He started farming in the middle of the Great Depression and retired in the late 1970s. He was a bit of a cult hero in all the grandchildren's eyes because when we were young he took us up on his knee and informed us that he was the man that grew the crops that made beer possible: barley, hops, and so on.

He was a regular hero to my mother and her siblings. No one ever heard him speak a foul word about anyone. He was the consummate neighbor and community man, treating every neighboring farmer's problems and harvest as if it were his own. He was gentle in spirit but as strong as a North Dakotan blizzard breeze.

Sylvester worked through floods and tornadoes, as well as depressions, recessions, and crises of every sort. He worked long hours and months and lived modestly, saved what he could, and sold his farm to move to town at age 67. When he died, he left a sizeable inheritance to his four children, one of whom was my mother.

"When I think of how hard he worked and how quickly I lost what he worked so hard to get, it just shames me," Mom continued. "Some of those years were so difficult. I remember the flood and Daddy losing the entire crop. I sit and think about which years I just lost. Was it 1938 to 1943? Was it 1955 to 1960? I feel so bad about it."

Mom's intention in calling me that day was to ask my help and guidance in selecting a new financial advisor. She needed someone she could trust and was clueless as to where to turn after the experience with her "friend."

I knew that, at the very least, Mom needed an advisor who measured money the same way she did.

## How the Industry Measures Money

An advisor friend called me after exiting a sales meeting with his branch manager. He was distraught. Dave believes in putting the interests of his clients first. He's the kind of guy who measures money the way my mother does.

"Mitch, I can't believe that some people still want to try to conduct business this way. Haven't we learned anything as a company?" Dave lamented.

Dave went on to describe that Monday morning's pep talk from his manager. "We need to get these numbers moving," he said, "and here's just the product to do it." He went on to deliver a piquant pitch on the product of the week that had a payout for the advisor of 5.85 percent. "Now you ought to be able to stir some business with *that*," he charged them. The *that* in this rallying cry being self-interest with a shot of steroids, not the quality of the product at hand.

"I walked out of there thinking, 'What does my getting 585 basis points have to do with the well-being of my client?'" Dave continued, "Sure, that product might fit somebody in my book, but that is not the proper premise for me to be calling them—so I can stick a little more money in my pocket whether the shoe fits them or not."

## AUM and EGO

*Assets under management* is the mantra of the annuitized book of business for the individual advisor and the bedrock of staying power for the financial institution. It should not surprise us that this business model comes with its own peculiar conflicts, the principal conflict being firmly rooted in the advisor's ego and reputation.

Many firms touted the model of AUM as being client friendly, client centric and a few other unselfish euphemisms. Instead of making commissions on the sale of particular products, the conventional wisdom touted, advisors were now seated on the same side of the table as the client, winning when the client won and losing when the client lost.

This is akin to the railroad's saying to the grain elevator, "Instead of charging you each time you rent a car, we will charge you by the pound to ship your grain, so it's in our best interest to make sure that your grain arrives safely."

"No doubt," the merchant might muse, "but the railroad will be paid for the cargo they carry no matter how much the rats eat." Assets under management in one respect is like being paid to carry freight, except for the fact that the client has an expectation that the freight will grow by the time it reaches its destination. At the end of the day, however, in the AUM model, the advisor is paid on the freight aboard.

In the industry transition to AUM, the measure for "production" success moved from "commissions earned" to "assets under management." Egos will rise to whatever measure is produced to measure their worth. You'd have to be blind to not note the relationship between AUM and reputation in this industry. Yesterday's "top producer" was the person earning the most commissions, which may have come from churning. Today's "top producer" is the person gathering the most assets.

My advisor friend may well have been speaking the truth to me. He told me that his firm had moved to an AUM approach and that the impact on his business was, in his words: "I'm now looking out for the interest of my clients, more than ever." It might have been my imagination, but it seemed like the words *more than ever* weren't quite in rhythm with the rest of his statement.

"Before," he said, "with commissions, you were always tempted to make a sale without knowing if it was really the right thing. With this approach, I'm on the same side of the table as my clients."

"And," he added with a grin, "I get a regular check every month for about $30k."

If you read any industry publications, you cannot help but notice the pattern of quoting advisors first by name and second by assets under management, for example, "The opinion of Jake Renshaw, CFP ($159 AUM), from Stargate Advisors in Akron, Ohio, is that . . ."

This style of notation does a fine job of arousing egos and infers that the only people with valid opinions are those with a minimum of $X under management. Companies across the industry measure the advisor's efficacy by same standard. I understand that numbers are typically good indicators of success, but they do fail to tell the whole story. In terms of efficacy, an advisor in St. Cloud, Minnesota, with $30 million AUM may be thrice the talent that an advisor in Seattle with $300 million AUM is, given the opportunity, demographics, and localized economic potential. Yet the two will be treated as if they belong to two different caste systems in many organizations, thus arousing the ego in a way that cannot possibly be in the best interest of the client.

There are those advisors who have chosen to do a magnificent job for a select few clients. They have impeccable relationships with the clients they serve but will never appear on the "president's council" or any other "what have you done for me lately?" ranking.

These are not inferior advisors, just people who have found a sweet spot that fits them in business and life. It's time for firms to take notice of this soulish reality of our times.

I know advisors with gazillions under management who are both brilliant and full of integrity, and I know those with gazillions under management who are so full of themselves that it is a physiological wonder that there is room for any vital organs or, for that matter, one bit of concern for their client.

On the other end of the spectrum, I know advisors who have what the industry would characterize as "negligible" assets under management who are brilliant and full of integrity, as well as those in the same boat who are bumbling incompetents. We don't measure the best doctors by the sum of the money they make but by the quality of their work; it is their reputation that sells. If the doctor does quality work, there is a very good chance he will be in the top quartile of the earnings chart, but, then again, his earnings could be determined by the nature of his discipline, be it pediatrics or cardiology. It's unlikely that the absolute best in the former cannot approach the least competent in the latter in terms of earning power.

The Mayo Clinic employs some of the most brilliant physicians, surgeons, and researchers in the world who work for wages that are minor factors of what they could make in more "enterprising" environments. But they do so knowingly, with a transcending desire to serve the public as well as serve among the brightest minds in their field. I see this as an allegory of certain trends among advisors who desire to serve in the realm of "wealth care"—advisors who are weary of the brokerdealer cajoling for greater "production." This breed of advisor cannot be ignored, as the clientele they attract is loyal to them and has more staying power than the clientele of the archetype financial services salesman.

Money under management cannot be the final measure of success. Sooner or later, this industry will find a measure that is a truer indicator of serving clients well, but I suspect we are at least a score of full moons away from that day, which leads to the query, "Is there a way to measure clients' assets and measure an advisor's success that are synchronous and void of compromise?"

When I juxtapose the two phone calls I experienced, the first with Mom and the second with Dave, I sense that what might be missing in financial services at large and in advisors individually, could be summed up in one word: *empathy*.

See the world from your client's point of view. View the proposition from your client's perspective. Examine the options from your client's vantage point. Measure money the way your client measures money, not in digits that end in zeros but in the price that was paid to obtain it.

"Do you appreciate the price I paid to get this $200,000 as much as the $2,000 annual drip that I hold before you?" the client could well be wondering. With empathy in the lead chair, it wouldn't really matter whether it was $2 million or $20,000 sitting before you. Empathy simply respects the price that was paid to harvest it.

## An Empathic View

Your client trades his life for the money he brings to you. He trades his talents, energies, aptitudes, potential, and, most significantly, his time, which comes from a limited and unreplenishable account.

Some of your clients have traded their marriages and relationships with their children for the assets they gathered and will begin to animate regret, both emotionally and economically, over this fact as they age. Does the empathic advisor, who has heard the story of the price that was paid, have an advantage in this soul-driven marketplace? I believe that she does.

What dreams and what essence of who they feel they really are did your client sacrifice to achieve the material wealth that they grip with all the strength in their hands? Every one pays a price of one sort or another.

There is a need to get the story of how that wealth was formed before we can experience true empathy. I would have not sympathized as deeply for my mother's loss had her loss been described strictly in numerical digits. Math is not the language of the soul. Real, veritable empathy was formed when I heard her loss described in the blood, sweat, and tears of her father. After all, it was he who gathered this harvest. What digit can begin to tell this tale? Every one of your clients has a tale of some sort, of assets gotten, assets bought, assets labored for, and assets lost.

Martin, an advisor who lives in my city, called me one day and offered to buy me lunch, assuring me that he only wanted to tell me a story that he was sure would be of interest to me. After we ordered our lunch at the local T.G.I. Friday's, he opened with,

"Some months ago I read a piece you wrote about understanding the pain or the price that was paid in possessing the asset brought for investment gain. The idea stuck with me and I realized, in being honest with myself, that although I cared very much for my clients' well-being, I knew very little of this side of the money story. I resolved that I would ask a simple question whenever a client put a check in front of me, the question being, "What does this money represent to you?"

Martin went on to tell about a conversation that forever altered his view of client assets: "The very first client that came in after I had resolved this within myself laid a check down that he had received from an insurance company for over $400,000. I asked him, 'What does this money represent to you?' His answer pinned me against my chair.

"'It represents nine months of my life in traction, and don't you dare lose one penny of it,'" was the answer Martin heard.

"It's hard," Martin said to me, "to realize that you've had a gaping hole in your strategy for building client relationships, and it makes you wonder how much opportunity you've missed because of this hole in your awareness, but I think I've learned my lesson."

Thanks for lunch, Martin.

## The Search for Meaning

A very simple question any advisor can ask to begin experiencing this quality of empathy with each client is, *"Can you tell me story of how this wealth was formed?"*

Unless the client sitting across from you is a member of the Mafia or a drug runner, they will thoroughly enjoy the opportunity to share with you the price that was paid to earn the money in question. People love to tell such stories but are rarely offered the opportunity. If nothing else, they certainly remember—positively—advisors who ask such questions by showing interest in them beyond their assets.

You will hear stories of opportunities lost and gained. You'll hear stories of sacrifice and risk and of ventures and dreams. You'll hear stories of parents and children and hardship and pain. You'll hear stories of entrepreneurial windfalls and of safe and steady gains.

Enough advisors have taken me up on this challenge that I guarantee three things will happen as you hear these stories:

1. You will gain empathy for your client.
2. Your client will gain appreciation and trust for and with you.
3. A bridge of understanding will be built between the two of you.

How do we build that bridge of understanding and trust between the client who has been burned and the advisor who needs business to improve? We build that bridge with empathy. Empathy alone can bring the cure for what ails the industry at large and relationships individually.

We need to *hear* our client's story.

I mean *really* hear their story: empathy is formed, respect is established, and we are no longer tempted to do anything that puts our own interests ahead of the client we now know and understand in a manner that transcends our most desperate state.

## A New Measure

> *Still, as of old, men by themselves are priced. For thirty pieces Judas sold himself, not Christ.*
>
> —Hester H. Cholmondeley

The way we measure money will change when the way we measure people changes. I know many in this industry who measure people in digits (i.e., "That guy's worth a lot"), and no doubt they measure money the same way they measure people. But, I might ask, how do we usually measure people? The measure of a man or a woman is by their character, reputation, talents, efforts, and accomplishments—in that order.

By hearing the story of how your clients accumulated their wealth, you will get a more accurate measure of who they are, the price they have paid, and the kind of character, talent, and effort it took to create that wealth. Their story may impress you in a way that motivates you to serve them the very best you can, or it may dissuade you from wanting to serve them at all. But the story you hear will undoubtedly change your point of reference with that client.

I know that for my mother, I want an advisor who appreciates the toil, years, discipline, love of family, and love of the land that created the wealth she inherited from her father, the farmer. However, I want more than that. I want an advisor for my mother who also understands the price of entrepreneurial risk, vision, and daring that the daughter of this farmer displayed in her life and passed down to her children.

Come to think of it, that's the kind of advisor *I* want for myself and my family—the kind of advisor who, rather than telling me a story of what they will do with the money I bring, first wants the story of how the money came into my hands and the price I paid to get it. This is the truest measure of money.

### ReSOULution

Move beyond counting money and become an expert in measuring it. Take advantage of every conversation with clients to build empathy regarding their wealth and all it represents. Don't just count the money: weigh it, measure it with your soul.

# CHAPTER 11

# Spinning Out of Control

*Plenty of people miss their share of happiness, not because they never found it, but because they didn't stop to enjoy it.*
—William Feather

*We should revel in our electronically supercharged, unbounded world. But, to make the most out of this new world, to avoid feeling overbooked, overstretched, and about to snap, to make modern life become better than life has ever been, a person must learn how to do what matters most first.*
—Edward M. Holowell

Our lives spin along at incredible rates of speed, filling us with a need for a gravitational force, one that we hope will keep us grounded. That gravitational force comes from people who give us a sense of meaning—wives and husbands, sons and daughters, mothers and fathers, preachers and rabbis, philosophers and guides. I have always hoped to be such a person. I see far too many lives spinning around the axis of work and orbiting around a source of light that, frankly speaking, has too few watts and will eventually leave those lives in the dark.

Because our lives and our clients' lives move so quickly (too quickly), we need time and space to step out of the axis of work/ life to just breathe, to pull out of the orbit around which our life revolves and just think. I have always been moved by couples celebrating their 50th year together who said, "Where did the time go?" and by men and women at their retirement parties wistfully reflecting, "It all happened so *fast.*"

## When Spin and Orbit Rates Are Out of Sync

In a business that is primarily concerned with how we invest our money, it might do us good to reflect on the larger question of how we invest our time. Money is invested in the larger context of time; that is, *I invest this money in the hopes of owning my time and being able to do something meaningful with it.*

The *spin* rate in our lives is something we should reflect on and decide to do something about. Time keeps on moving whether we want it to or not, but what we *do* with that time is our decision. The spin rate in our lives (the thing that feels like our head is spinning at 1,000 mph) revolves around the axis of our daily activity. The question many need to ponder is whether that activity is energizing or enervating. One fills you up and the other leaves you flattened. Many working lives are a combination of the two, double espresso with a depressive chaser.

It is estimated that at least 16.5 million Americans practice yoga as a means for managing stress, promoting health, and creating a more meaningful life. At what point do we examine the lifestyle that put us in this tied-up state and treat the cause instead of the symptom?

Far too many working lives are just plain depressing because of their all-consuming nature and the fact that they work against who we are as a person. Many, instead of being authentic versions of who they are, settle for being second-rate versions of what some company wants them to be.

Far too few are living lives that are purely energizing.

The *orbit* rate in our lives (the thing that makes us feel that we are moving at 66,000 mph) has to do with our *rasion d'être* and the long-term sense of meaning and value we feel we add or subtract with those activities. Our lives are spinning and orbiting synchronously, spinning with short-term activity while they rotate with long-term significance. It is when the spin (the daily tasks) and/or the orbit (the purpose for doing the tasks) is out of sync with who we are that we feel we are losing control of our existence, that our lives are spinning out of control.

We are just such a nation and culture.

A report in *CIO* magazine stated that executives and senior managers work at least 50 hours a week. Many of those respondents indicated that those 50 hours did not include the late-night and weekend juggling of phone calls, e-mails, paperwork, and computer-based project work. Each electronic advance, such as cell phones, e-mail, personal digital assistants (PDAs), and the like, constricts our mid-section like a boa until we can no longer find breathing room. We no longer just go to the office. Now the office goes with us. "We just want to keep you in the loop" is really code for "You'd better check your e-mail tonight." So much for a relaxing evening with the family. Welcome to the world of the high-tech leash.

More and more people are wearing feelings of being over-worked like a red-eyed badge of courage. Workers one-up each other with stories about their busy lives. Sadly, our use of technology, instead of delivering on its promise to make life easier and less complicated, often compounds it.

This is but one of the many disturbing findings in the study, "Overwork in America: When the Way We Work Becomes Too Much," from the Families & Work Institute. Through telephone interviews with 1,003 working adults, the study yielded a number of alarming results, including:

- Forty-four percent of U.S. employees often or very often feel overwhelmed by how much they have to do at work.
- Overworked employees are more likely to feel angry at work and resent coworkers who don't work as hard as they do.
- Technology use adds to feelings of being overworked.

Let's focus on the impact of technology. It certainly has made us more efficient at work, giving us more ways to manage and save time. It has enhanced our creativity beyond what many thought possible. But therein lays the double-edged sword. As much as technology has enabled us to do, it also adds to the overwork dilemma in which many U.S. workers, particularly professionals, are feeling trapped.

Consider these additional study findings:

- Thirty-three percent of employees were in contact with work once a week or more outside of normal work hours.
- Fifty-six percent of employees experience one or both of the following:
  - ◆ Too many tasks at the same time.
  - ◆ Too many interruptions.
- Eighty-nine percent of employees feel they never have enough time to get everything done.

According to senior economist Jared Bernstein of the Economic Policy Institute in Washington, "Over the last 30 years, middle-income couples with kids have added an average of 20 weeks of work, the equivalent of five months a year." Bernstein's remarks illustrate the compression of personal time that takes place when fathers who have always worked a lot of hours continue to work many hours but are now joined in the workplace by mothers, who once stayed home.

According to a study by the Pew Research Center, 26 percent of American women say they always feel rushed during their day compared with 21 percent of men. Working women, however, are feeling under the weight of a constant time pressure, with 33 percent saying they are rushed all the time.

If it is true of middle-income workers, it is all the more true of higher-income managers and executives. The more money you take home, the more time you are expected to devote to your professional life. Higher pay doesn't free the modern executive—it just influences the composition of metal used to forge his or her shackles, be it steel or gold.

Many of your most successful and prosperous clients are cases in point:

Linda is the youngest and only female executive in her corporation. Because of this, she feels she has something to prove at all times. She has trouble relaxing. Her definition of relaxing is working a 12-hour day instead of 16 hours. When she does "relax," she encounters the tacit disapproval of her long-divorced, workaholic CEO who believes that a 16-hour day is the benchmark of "executive dedication." He has no problem with the way his world is spinning.

He has little time for reflecting on the fact the sun around which his world has orbited is "making a fortune and rising to the top" and that somehow all the important people in his life have been thrown off of his world as it spins at 1,000 miles an hour and orbits at 66,000 miles an hour around a *faux lumière,* a false light.

Linda sometimes feels like her world is spinning too fast and that there just isn't enough time for the important things. Like 90 percent of her fellow Americans, she would like to throttle back a degree or two and restore a sense of balance and control in her life. The fact that her health was seriously threatened recently compounded her dilemma. She told me how she was offered an executive position at a competitor at twice the pay and a "normal" eight-hour workday, but she couldn't take it because the firm making the offer had serious integrity issues. She wasn't willing to seek balance at the expense of who she is. So her life rotation and orbit continues at a dizzying pace.

## The Spoils of Success

Peter called me on my cell phone as I was walking through security at an airport. I asked him to bear with me as I laid the phone on the X-ray conveyer. While the phone and I passed inspection, I processed the troubled tone in Pete's voice: I knew instantly what it was I had detected in his tone: lamentation—disillusionment with success (like Solomon of old in the Book of Proverbs asking us to sympathize with the vacuous space left by worldly success). I was familiar with this tone from my early days in suicide prevention work. In the course of the conversation that ensued, he confessed that the spin of his professional life and the long-term rotation of his orbit had left him in a depressive funk that he was medicating with alcohol and thoughts of ending it all.

We had many conversations after that, which forced him to start examining the objective around which he wanted his life to orbit and then examining how congruent the spin of his daily life was with that desired orbit. When both the rotation and orbit of his daily existence were put in alignment with who he was, a new sense of meaning entered his life. He now sees how he can add value to every life he touches in his work. He has new energy and passion, and it shows in his family life and in his work life.

Somebody told Peter, and Peter told himself that it was all about the money and about moving up the ladder. Nobody told him how insecurity grows with every step up a ladder or how precarious life is at the top of that ladder. When you are at the top of a ladder, all you can think of is falling. There is nowhere else to go. The orbit around corporate objectives stole his soul and left him in perpetual darkness, like an Alaskan winter, with no hope of spring's ever appearing. When he looked up the ladder he was climbing, like Linda, he saw lives and schedules and priorities that gave him existential nausea.

You think you (or your client) want to be CEO? Think again. One study showed that over 60 percent of retired CEOs were depressed and disenchanted. For years they were too busy to notice that they had come unhinged from nature's orbit and had gone hurtling toward a black hole of existence. They had invested everything in something that had no power to pay them back. To make matters worse, they had neglected those who could pay them dividends in their post-CEO years.

## Restoring Balance to the Life Portfolio

Money is the means, and quality of life is the end. We all know this, but somehow and somewhere that money tail started wagging the dog in many of our lives. Down deep, we understand that we should be using our money to make a life and not using our life to make money, but it doesn't always work out that way, and it's not easy figuring out how to get the dog back.

How in the world did we find ourselves in the financial state we are in?

We took a job. We found a mate, and together we found a house. Soon we found out a baby was coming. We bought a bigger house. Maybe we got divorced. We had to sell the house and split time with the kids. We found a new mate. We bought a new and bigger house. Maybe we stretched a bit in the house we bought, but that's the price you pay to be in a good school district. Plus, we had been working hard and felt like we deserved some reward, which is also the reason we took the trips. And bought the new vehicle. And ran up the credit cards.

Now we realize that maybe this job is costing us more than it is paying us, but we can see no reasonable exit ramp. We're stuck. We created a lifestyle that cost a price that we never planned on paying, but that we must now perpetuate in order to continue paying the bills. We go to work in golden shackles, or maybe they're not even golden—just shackles.

We know we work too much and that our lives are out of balance. We know we buy things we don't need with money we don't have. We know that we are a slave to those we owe. We know that our children grow up much too quickly and that we'll never get these years back. We know that we have sacrificed important parts of who we are for the things we thought we wanted to get. We are a tired and unbalanced people. It is what we do with our time that makes us unbalanced, but it is what we know—but do not do—that makes us so very tired.

At some point, we must step back from this madness of exhausting the best parts of who we are for things that mold and dust can corrupt. We have all walked through this reflection, some of us many times. Now is the time to do something about it. Life is not a dress rehearsal, and money is a poor substitute for a sense of purpose.

Money is not, in fact, our most valuable resource.

Of all manageable earthly resources, time is exponentially more valuable than money and ought to be the head rather than the tail in the process of designing a life that works. People complain about not having time to do the things they want. Why? Is it because these people have chosen to spend their time in an activity that does not satisfy them? Why do they do this? Is it because these same people have mortgaged their ability to fully utilize their energy and abilities for the shackles of material acquisition?

It is our time that matters and how well we invest that time is the real subject here. Karen Salmansohn and Don Zinzell, the authors of *How to Be Happy, Dammit: A Cynic's Guide to Spiritual Happiness* (Celestial Arts, 2001) say in Life Lesson #40: "It's not 'he who dies with the most toys wins.' It's 'he who has the most time to play with his toys and the most fun playing with them who wins.'" Once we settle on how we want to invest our time, the topic of how we want to invest our money takes on a whole new meaning, the sort of meaning and context that a financial advisor would do well to surface in client conversations.

## Your Desired Life Portfolio

I designed the client conversation tool, Your Life Portfolio™ (see Figure 11.1) to assist advisors in helping clients get at this sense of meaning for their money. Advisors around the country inform

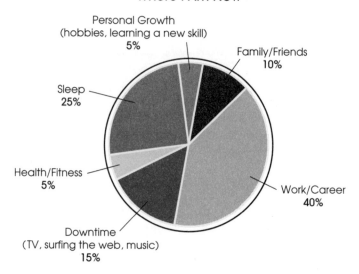

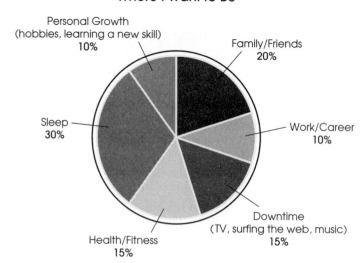

**Figure 11.1   Your Life Portfolio™**

me that this tool creates a powerful context for making investment decisions and taking decisive action. Why? Because people want to do something to change their paradigm from "using their life to make money" to "using their money to make a life."

In this conversation tool, I have used asset allocation as a metaphor for our most critical life allocation: *how we invest our time.* Everyone has 168 hours a week to invest. How are you spending that time right now? The client fills out their allocation and the software produces a pie chart like the one in the figure. The first thing that jumps out at most clients is the blaring red siren of work and the death of verdant family green and tranquil leisure blue. We then ask them fill out their Desired Life Portfolio™. Once this is filled out, the advisor makes the commitment to help them organize their money in a way that causes their Desired Life Portfolio to materialize and continue. The investment planner is now a vital facilitator in the self-actualization process in a way that would make Abraham Maslow blush with satisfaction.

But you must first invest in your client's life before expecting your client to invest with you. You invest in your clients by inquiring into their working lives and discovering what their ultimate work-life goal looks like. Many of your clients are at their wits' end with their working lives. They have no balance and don't know when or where they'll find it. Their money is an integral piece of this conversation, but it is not the lead piece. Money is the supporting actor in the drama of their work life.

## Light Years Ahead

There will always be night and day, but when it is dark for months and years at a time, it's time to examine both our axis *and* orbit. How we invest our time and the reason we spend it as we do are the most pressing investment issues facing Americans today. If you can engage in this sort of dialogue, your clients will have no reservations about asking you to manage their money—as long as your suggestions and advice support their desired life portfolio. You bring light to the situation simply by inquiring into what their desired scenario might be and jump-starting the strategizing process.

I was surprised when I learned how rapidly the earth rotated: 1,000 miles per hour. It certainly doesn't feel as though it's moving that fast. It's the amazing power of gravity that keeps our footing secure. I was doubly amazed to learn how rapidly the earth orbits the sun: 66,000 miles per hour. It doesn't seem possible that we could be moving at that rate of speed (100 times the speed of sound), but we are.

Whether we sense it or not, our lives are moving that quickly.

As a professional, you ought to examine both your daily rotation and your long-term orbit. When these two—your activity and purpose—are in synchronicity, you will be both an example and inspiration to your clients. You may find yourself doing more than just giving financial advice: you may find yourself giving advice that keeps clients' lives from spinning out of control.

---

### ReSOULution

Take the time to examine your time budget. Are you chasing it, losing it, or investing it? Does your expenditure of time drain you more than it fills you? The sands of time fall whether we pay attention or not. We have an opportunity to pay attention and to adjust our time to fit our souls, and thus lead more fulfilled lives.

# 12

# Protecting Your Clients From *Halfluence*

*The successful companies of the twenty-first century will be the ones satisfying emotional needs.*

—Rolf Jensen

*Gossip is about rich people having problems money can't solve.*

—Aaron Spelling

Mike and Annie are affluent. They fit the description of the clients you want and believe you can help. Mike, in his early 40s, and Annie, in her late 30s, are extremely talented and likeable people. They both have been collecting six-figure salaries for over a decade and have saved considerable sums in their retirement programs—and live well within their means. They live in a beautiful home that resides in an exclusive and gated suburban neighborhood.

There is only one factor contradicting their affluence: their lifestyles are stealing from them more than they are gaining. They hate going to work and working for "semi-psychotic" and "professionally dishonest" people who represent companies that they know would throw both of them on the woodpile in the time it takes to strike a match, should it serve their bottom-line interests to do so. Mike and Annie—and many like them who have shared their stories with me in the last year—have seen their share of megalomaniacal managers who would be given DUIs if anyone were policing the power trip. They have witnessed the dark side of the "Peter Principle," as inept people get promoted to the level of their own incompetence and actually start believing that there is a garden growing in their pea-sized brains. Never mind the fact that a 10- to 12-hour day, once exceptional, now appears to be the minimally acceptable standard of corporate devotion.

Mike and Annie, and others like them, don't so much come home as they do fall through the door, burned black every day like a piece of toast from a temperamental toaster. Too black to scrape and salvage, they just throw it away—only it's not just a piece of bread being discarded, it's another day, the bread of life.

By the end of each week they have nothing left for *their* life—a social life, adventure, and just going out and having fun. They are depleted like the cheap batteries that come with the break-within-the-hour holiday gifts. They have nothing left after five long days of burnt toast. They sit around all weekend and slowly recharge and think and talk and dream about how great it would be to pick up that toaster and hurl it with all their might against the wall. There. It's done. No more burnt toast. A six-figured, white-collared version of Johnny Paycheck's "Take this job and shove it!"

Listening to their story and knowing them as I do, I must believe them. They are hardworking, honest people who don't like pulling down the shades on their hearts every day before work. Their personal health has been showing wear and tear the last couple of years, no doubt from the cumulative effect. The immune system hasn't yet figured out how to counteract a conflicted life.

They remind me of those students in an old-time school who went to class every day knowing they are going to be berated and humiliated by the teacher who has no business teaching but does. They also know that occasionally, when they question things in the classroom, the teacher will grab them by the hair and pull them down to the principal's office. In the principal's office they are given their checks, and they are very big checks. "These checks are big enough," the tacit understanding goes, "that you have no business complaining about how you must go about collecting them."

They have cashed these checks and bought themselves a cage—a gilded cage—shiny yet confining. They are reminded of the constraints of this cage every time they think of something they would rather be doing.

The concept of golden handcuffs (remember our discussion in the previous chapter) has become so common it has even made it into the dictionary:

> gold·en hand·cuffs. a series of raises, bonuses, etc., given at specified intervals or tied to length of employment so as to keep an executive from leaving the company. (*Random House Unabridged Dictionary,* Copyright © 1997)

A question to ponder, then, is this: If a device were applied to inhibit your freedom, what would matter most to you over time? The fact that the device choked off your liberty or the composition/value of the device?

Think this scenario is uncommon? Think again. Professional people fitting the Mike and Annie story number in the hundreds of thousands. I hear their stories everywhere I go. If the financial services profession is going to have any relevance in these people's lives, it is going to have to first help them design an escape plan out of their cages.

## Getting Our Money's Worth

Many Americans are making more, but are they living better? Are we pursuing affluence but settling for *half*fluence? Studies show that the more we make, the less we sleep. In fact, we now sleep 90 minutes a less a night than our forebears did a century ago, and the alarm clock continues the setback a few minutes each year.

One study demonstrated that men working 60 hours a week are twice as likely to have a heart attack as those who work 40 hours. Obesity rates are skyrocketing as American workers slam down high-calorie, processed foods and have no time or energy left for exercise. Can this be good for business? Are our corporations experiencing "*half*fluence" as well because of these trends? The American Institute of Stress reports that stress causes at least a million Americans to miss work every single working day at a cost to businesses of more than $300 billion a year. Fatigue on the

Figure 12.1    What Workers Say about Stress on the Job

job, probably causing more erosion on the bottom line than those not showing up, not only shipwrecked the *Exxon Valdez* but many a career as well (see Figure 12.1).

## Wake Me When It's Time to Go

It's not just the issue of stress that people often feel on the job, but the fact that they are taking it home with them and not sleeping well at night, and returning again to work in this fogged and wearied state.

"And the most worrisome part of this is these people don't realize how sleep-deprived they really are," lead researcher Hans P. A. Van Dongen, PhD, assistant professor of sleep and chronobiology at the University of Pennsylvania School of Medicine, tells WebMD. "When people are put through chronic sleep deprivation, there is an initial response where they say, 'OK, this is not optimal but I'll manage." But after a few days of this, things are much worse than they realize." *In other words, they actually become too tired to realize just how tired they are.* They may feel only a little tired, says Van Dongen, but they have slower reaction time, weakened memory, and other thinking impairments. His study, published in *Sleep,* adds to the growing list of health risks from sleep deprivation. It's not surprising that a 2007 study conducted by the researchers at Harvard Medical School and Boston's Beth Israel Deaconess Medical Center found that lack of sleep seriously impairs our memory. Other research studies have found that that regularly getting too little sleep boosts heart disease risk, and can contribute to a higher risk of diabetes and obesity.

And when is showing up a sign of stressing out? How about when you are afraid to take a vacation for fear of things falling apart, or someone's messing things up, or someone's realizing they really don't need you that much?

Americans left $60.4 billion dollars in vacation days on their employers' table in 2006—and the number keeps increasing each year. That's the total dollar value of the amount of vacation time remanded back to employers last year by American workers, according to Expedia.com's annual Vacation Deprivation™ survey. The survey also estimated that American workers relinquished 439 million vacation days.

> *Problems at work are more strongly associated with health complaints than are any other life stressor—more so than even financial problems or family problems.*
> —St. Paul Fire and Marine Insurance Co.

## In Better Company

Some companies are beginning to figure out this problem, according to Carl Honorè, author of *In Praise of Slowness: How a Worldwide Movement Is Challenging the Cult of Speed.* He cites the example of SAS Software in Cary, North Carolina, which combines a 35-hour workweek with generous vacation benefits—and has strong profits and has been listed in the top 10 of *Fortune's* "Best Companies to Work For."

The Best Buy Corporation in Minneapolis, Minnesota, implemented a program for executives and managers where they are officially "off the clock" and measured simply by virtue of productivity.

They are free to work at home, in their pajamas or at any hours they see fit, as long as they get the job done. The early results are showing significantly higher production from the now-happier, working-at-home executives.

This approach might be working in North Carolina and in Minnesota, but I wouldn't hold my breath for a similar approach if I were working in New York, Los Angeles, or anywhere else the boardrooms are filled with worshippers at the First Church of the Bean Counter and members of the Cult of Speed.

*Half*fluence has not yet expired its half-life in America, but the trend for wholeness will continue. Witness the renaissance of the "slow down, enjoy the moment, I have a life" approach to life. In the past five years, over 4 million Americans under the age of 35 have taken up hobbies like gardening, reading, and even knitting. Maybe the post-boom generation has beaten the baby boomers to the realization that a meditative state is preferable to a medicated state.

But in the land of *half*fluence, careers fueled by fear and adrenaline will continue to fall into their weekly weekend collapse.

## A New Way of Measuring Wealth

My friend, Lewis Walker, a renowned financial planner in Atlanta and great thinker on money/meaning issues, sent me these words, "Money can by you position but not respect, it can buy you a clock but not time, it can buy you medicine but not health, . . ." and so on. These words suggested to me that we are entering a time where money is no longer the measure of affluence for the clients we serve.

Lew suggests an economy of fulfillment that is measured by something he calls *"Boomer*nomics." I think he has something here. Signs of *Boomer*nomics are all around us and are not exclusive to boomers. The bookend generations (third-agers and the savvy gen-Xers) have taken notice as well, either through experience or observation, of the impotence of the hard-charging, worship-the-corporate-beast, and burn-the-candle and burnout-the-body lifestyle.

I was recently talking to senior management of a firm that had moved its headquarters to the suburbs 20 years ago to attract all the talented suburbanites. They are now facing tremendous difficulty recruiting younger talent because these people live in the city and are tired of the drive out and back everyday, and so they have opted to work for the competition that has offices closer to where they live. They want a life and a job. What a novel concept.

This is one trend of many that points to the mature realization that the payday does not guarantee the payoff. Americans are also beginning to assess how much those paychecks are *costing* them—the trade-offs of energy, irretrievable time, and demands upon them that they have bartered for their pay stubs.

They are beginning to see that, even with higher wages and growing investments, they are not necessarily *getting their money's worth*. There is something that today's advisor can do about it, but first, a change in how we measure success is necessary.

## Measure What Money Can Buy

Instead of directing clients to measure success by return on investment (ROI), we could be encouraging them to measure "return on life" (ROL). How well are we utilizing their money to improve their quality of life? What level of emotional dividend is each of your clients experiencing with their money? Many Americans are experiencing emotional losses while their balances are climbing. *This is the financial industry's next great challenge—amalgamating life and wealth into an integral discussion that eradicates the demarcation between account balances and balance in life.*

Many veterans of the wealth management business acknowledge the phenomenon of *half*fuence among the wealthy and are beginning to offer a "Well-th Being" approach to the high-net-worth marketplace.

One executive cited the Service Corporation of America as an example of how a provider can transform itself from transactional to transformational. The Service Corporation of America used to be in the business of selling caskets and burying dead bodies, but now acts as a biographer and celebrant of the life of the individual who "has left us for the time being." They came to the realization that their commoditized industry and shrinking margins could not be rescued by faster, better, or cheaper, but instead must be revolutionized by finding the best location in the market of emotion. Their value-added proposition is now the casket/burial, etc., which adds to the greater value of memorializing.

The financial services industry has been selling affluence but delivering *half*fluence. We can change that. If the mortuary industry can transform itself from being undertakers to posthumous biographers and celebrants of life, I would hope that the financial services industry could begin to offer a superior experience to what it has been offering. But to do so will mean moving the focus away from the physical, tangible product and service to the emotional endgame for the client. And rest assured, your success will pivot on how well acquainted you are with your clients' story—a story that they want to bring to life with their money. Think of their stories as unproduced movie scripts that will be brought to the big screen with the right executive producer and director. Can you play the role of executive producer—the person who puts up the money in order to get the picture done?

Why should they wait until they're dead to get their stories told? You can act as their biographer while they are living and assist them in using their money to bring that story to life. This is what it means to achieve affluence. Not only are you getting rich, you are living rich as well.

Your clients want more than just financial advice—and the financial services profession is just now beginning to figure out what that something more is—*meaning*. It is fulfillment. It is balance. From an existential point of view, those who have come to a place of means now feel the need to move to a place of meaning. (This is true of everyone but those who are drowning out the sound of that need with the clatter of greed). Those with success want to move to significance. Money, without the freedom to pursue the things that fuel the feeling of meaning, will never buy anything more than *half*fluence.

The theory of marginal utility demonstrates that money means more to those who don't have it and less to those who do have it. If you have four slices of bread, one more makes a big difference. But if you have *four hundred* slices of bread, one more means nothing (which also goes a long way in explaining unreasonable greed—a little more no longer satisfies).

Richard Easterlin, a USC economist, surveyed 1,500 people over three decades to see what puts a genuine and lasting smile on their faces. His results, published in the *Proceedings for the National Academy of Sciences,* revealed that wealth doesn't necessarily lead to joy and contentment. One reason: People with more money usually want more things. According to Easterlin, the effect on subjective well-being of a $1,000 increase in income becomes progressively smaller the higher the initial level of income.

This phenomenon is what scientists call the "hedonic treadmill"—how the acquisition of commodities and clout provides a short-term emotional lift that makes us want more. We get a raise, spend it, the extra dough becomes moot, and we want more. When we look to money for happiness and get more money, we end up with *half*fluence. Where does it end? Is there a level of wealth that can exempt you from *half*fluence? Apparently not. University of Illinois psychologist Ed Diener found in his studies that the *Forbes* 400 wealthiest Americans are, for all intents and purposes, the same as Maasai herdsmen of East Africa.

From the vantage point of seeking a meaningful existence, I believe that it is the discussion of how this acquired abundance translates into abundant living that matters most to the soul of the client.

> *Take a look at your conventional overstuffed garage. Paradoxically, affluence has not led to fulfillment.*
>
> —Daniel H. Pink

Money can help your happiness—but only when properly utilized. Without proper utility, no amount of money in the world can rescue you from the futility and fruitlessness of doing things you hate with people you loathe or doing things that bore you and mortgaging precious months and years into that boredom.

Herein we find the roots of *half*fluence in America: what happens when I give everything I have for everything I can get, and it doesn't give back? The investment newsletters say I'm affluent but I'm fried. It's time to move our discussion with clients from the proper growing of assets to the proper utilization of those assets toward an optimal ROL. Return on life is the only veritable mark of affluence.

## Making Clients Rich and Enriching Clients' Lives

Do you know any individuals whose wallets are overflowing but look as though their souls have been drained in the process (the closer to money, the further from wealth)? Mike, and Annie—their eyes float before my memory like a train of affluent futility. They know they are going somewhere, sleeping in the finest accommodations, eating the best food, and drinking the best wine, but inside they are wondering if there is any way off this track. They like the accommodations but seriously doubt if this train can get them to where they want to go.

There is something they want. I see it in their eyes. No one has yet helped them to define it, to bring it to the conscious level, to articulate it, and to begin to live with a purposeful gait toward it. That something is meaning and balance. Intuitively, skilled advisors know how to build a bridge between their clients' means and sense of meaning—and between their account balances and sense of balance.

I also think that the financial advisor who has had the conversation with the Mikes and Annies of the world is going to be best positioned to help when they decide to make a change (and they will) at the point where their money is in motion.

At the end of the day when all the pay stubs are piled up, your clients will turn their focus from what they have gathered to what they have gained. It is at that moment that they will experience the chasm—the distance—between having made it and having it made.

## ReSOULution

You can love money all you wish, but it won't love you back. Choose objects for love that can return your affection. Don't let abundance get in the way of abundant living. Bring yourself to the happy place where you want what you already have, both for yourself and for your clients.

# 13

# The End of Retirement
# as We Know It

*How dull it is to pause, to make an end*
*To rust unburnish'd, to not shine in use*
*As tho' to breathe were life!*
　　　　　　—Alfred Lord Tennyson, "Ulyssess"

*It's never too late to be what you might have been.*
　　　　　　　　　　　　　—George Eliot

Imagine being a blacksmith 100 years ago. You had prospered in your business for many years because you provided an indispensable service to your community's chief transportation system. One day you look up and see a loud contraption that people are calling the "horseless carriage" coming down the main street. "Huh?" you think. "That will be the day!" and back to work you go. Ten years later your business is half of what it once was, and 20 years later it no longer exists. You, the blacksmith, failed to recognize one psychological key in succeeding with consumers: *If there is a more efficient way to live our lives, we will choose it even if it presents a whole new set of challenges.* Many a blacksmith probably discounted the motorized contraption as too complicated, problematic, and unproven for the majority of consumers to adopt.

Markets for popular products don't dry up overnight. The shift starts as a slow trickle, gains current slowly, and years later, reaches a rushing torrent. Successful merchants keep fluid mind-sets as they watch trends develop and adapt their goods and services to them. The wise merchant 100 years ago would have expanded his business to include repairing horseless carriages as well as shoeing horses. This expansion would have been accompanied by a new learning curve on the workings of gasoline engines. Those who simply kept their nose to the grindstone with the same offering of goods and services were one day replaced by a new breed of mechanic.

Allow me to share a montage of recent observations and conversations around retirement as we no longer know it. The mosaic that forms from these stories reveals a radical shift in the "third age" of life—formerly known as the "retirement years"—and, for you "wise merchants," an opportunity to position your practice for the new reality.

- I went out for dinner with Dick and Gail, a writer and an architect, respectively, in their 50s. Gail shared the story of how she transitioned away from a top firm to work for herself out of her home. Her reason for doing so? "I can't see myself working 50 to 60 hours a week anymore. By doing less of it, I enjoy it more. As a matter of fact, after two months, it dawned on me that I love my work so much that I can see doing this when I'm 80." Dick is a writer, full of ideas, and the idea of "retiring" sounds about as inviting as carbon monoxide poisoning. These two have their minds wrapped more around "rewiring" or "refiring," but certainly not retiring. Work, they understand, is not the problem. It's the hours and the company demands they want to prune away.
- A local merchant who ran a successful tire shop for three decades and retired at 65 opened a new store a year later. His back-in-business advertising campaign read, "I'm back in business because 'retirement sucks.'"
- Mercy Health Systems is well known for going out of its way to embrace older workers by providing meaningful work and allowing for a balanced life.
- Home Depot announced a national hiring campaign of "retirees" (coordinated with AARP). The rationale for the campaign? "They know more and they sell more."

Welcome to the dawning of the Experience Age, where gray hair indicates gray matter and the smart players in capitalist marketplace realize the errors of their "youth-seeking" ways. Home Depot's move is an initial flare in what will become a firestorm of exploiting the commercial value of experience and wisdom. This sort of value doesn't come in 25-year-old containers.

With the assistance of consulting firm CultureRX, corporations (like Best Buy, Inc. mentioned earlier) are allowing their key people to go "off the clock" and design their own work life at home, working when and how they want and being responsible only for getting results. The results? Higher productivity with those designing their own work life. Duh. What, no more commute? No more stupid time-burning meetings? Just get the job done on your terms? Who's going to want to retire from this? A whole lot fewer people from this crowd will be counting the days to the gold watch than from the clock-watching, meeting-maniacal group. Is Best Buy doing this because it's "the right thing to do"? You bet—employees are happier and more productive, the company is more profitable, and shareholders are content. Everyone wins.

## Removing "Tired" from Retired

Now, let's talk about your business. Are you a "retirement blacksmith" pounding out projections, or are you beginning to learn the modern skill sets of "Retirement Life Planning"? Are the goods and services you sell today as progressive as they were 10 or 15 years ago? Do they resonate with the way people want to order and live their lives? Years ago, people bought into the idea of a compartmentalized life course:

- The first part of your life you spend learning.
- The second part of your life you spend working and earning.
- The last part of your life (retirement) you spend in leisure or journeying.

This model for living is being rejected and rearranged for a more tailor-made design on life. Consider current trends that are evidence of this paradigm shift in life course navigation:

- Senior citizens are going back to college in record numbers. Thousands are "retiring" to university towns, instead of the traditional snowbird destinations.

- Many "retirees" are becoming entrepreneurs and reviving shelved dreams and passions.
- Many people in their prime earning years are taking steps back to be able to be present in their children's formative years. They feel they can make up for lost earnings when their children are grown, and they are no longer willing to sacrifice parental influence for immediate material advancement.
- Many people are rearranging their living circumstances in order to shift into more meaningful and fulfilling forms of work and less hectic lifestyles.
- Over 50 percent of retirees are going back to work after becoming bored with the prospects of full-time leisure.
- The idea of periodical "sabbaticals" from work is gaining popularity with high achievers and earners. They view these periods as necessary to reflect on their life direction. Morningstar offers all employees the opportunity to take a sabbatical, based on length of service.
- Adventure travel and learning vacations are popular with all age groups, especially the 50-plus crowd.
- The migration to the "sunbelt" is declining, and more people are retiring and becoming more involved in their own communities.

Next, add up the following demographic and societal changes and ask yourself what it means to your business going forward:

- According to the most recent U.S. Census (2000), the median age in the United States is 35, and is getting older every year.
- The workplace is facing a looming "brain drain" of managers and executives, and smart companies are beginning to offer "phased retirement" packages.
- Reversing a 50-year trend, the number of Americans working past age 65 is now rising.
- With companies cutting pensions and health benefits, many aging workers will not be able to afford to fully retire.
- With the repeal of the Social Security earnings restrictions, a major economic disincentive to working past age 65 has been removed.
- Many baby boomers continue their expensive indulgence— not wanting to wait until they are older to enjoy them.

- Seventy percent of baby boomers say they intend to continue work in some form during their "retirement."
- Forty-eight percent of Americans say they feel stressed because of finances; 24 percent cite health; and 32 percent cite employment issues.

What conclusions can you draw from the preceding facts and observations? What impact do you foresee in relation to the products and services you are selling, and the manner in which you are selling them? One question that begs asking is, "Is the traditional retirement planning process on the road to extinction?"

## The Times, They Are a-Changin'

Many people feel the concept of traditional retirement is hopelessly outdated and no longer applies to their lives. Many feel that the times have so radically changed that even the term *retirement* no longer applies. If people no longer connect with the concept or even the term *retirement,* how long will it take before they reject the process that leads to the concept they no longer embrace?

Rather than retiring, the 77 million baby boomers who began turning 59½ in 2005 are looking to a renaissance period of life. Are you prepared for the great rewiring boom that is ahead for your business? If you are still starting your "retirement" conversations with "How old are you and how much do you have?," you are going to miss the opportunity of a lifetime.

The graying boomer is not interested in retiring their "gray matter"—or their endorphins or sense of curiosity. Rather than reclining, they are redefining: looking for new mountains to climb; a new rhythm for their life; time to work, play, think, and explore. Do your conversations around retirement embrace this seismic cultural shift and help explore each client's potential and possibilities for the next 30 years of their life?

## Living Well

What does the retirement life planning conversation look like? I have developed the acronym LIVING W.E.L.L. as a guide:

**Work:** Doing what I enjoy most and want to start or continue with. Things I do well that bring value and meaning to my life.

**Equilibrium:** The need to keep a sane pace, create space for breathing and thinking, and to design a life in balance.

**Leisure:** Not full-time, but enough to keep fun and adventure in my life.

**Learning:** Keeping my mind sharp and challenged. Not only does mental acuity make me more interesting and interested, it offers hope for the future.

The advisor of the future is the person who can fulfill the role of wealth advisor with an eye toward wellness. To fulfill that role in your clients' lives, you'll need to abandon the hackneyed "retirement" worksheets and become lucid in the conversation outline above. Once the above has been defined, the final question your client will ask is, "How will we pay for this life?"

## Work with Me Here

The extended working life is being made possible by a confluence of factors that are physical, psychological, and intellectual in nature:

- People live longer today and many feel younger at older ages as a result. Remember, 65 is no longer old.
- People are beginning to view early retirement years as a "middle-escent" stage, where they can chase dreams in a childhood without supervision. Many retirees desire "re-creation" as much as recreation in their retirement years.
- "Knowledge capital" and experience, rather than physical labor, are the modern bargaining chips in the marketplace.
- Studies report on the importance of intellectual stimulation and purposeful pursuits in regard to successful aging.

None of these factors have escaped the attention of the boomer constituency. This is a group that has often frustrated the financial services industry with their free-spending, "live now" mentality. But this group, by and large, looks traditional retirement in the eye and sees it for what it is—an outdated concept that no longer fits.

In my book, *The New Retirementality*, I give a succinct history of how the idea of retirement got its start and how it established a foothold in American culture. The idea of governmentally institutionalized retirement first appeared in Germany in 1875 as introduced by Chancellor Otto Von Bismarck. At that time, the average male lived to age 46 and the retirement age was set at 65. The idea was imported by the FDR administration in 1935 as a way to put young men to work during the Great Depression. It was an appropriate idea in an industrial society where age had a significant bearing on output. Also motivating FDR was the fact that similar employment struggles in Italy and Germany had led to the rise in power of both Mussolini and Hitler. In 1935, the average worker lived to the age of 63 and the retirement age was set at 62.

It is clear in viewing the genesis of the traditional retirement model that the retirement journey was designed to last for 2 to 3 years, not 20 to 30. It was a short bridge from the factory loading dock to the eternal loading dock in those days.

If a person expected to live only to the age of 63 or so and retired at age 62, it may have made sense to fully indulge in a life of leisure and rest. But such full-time pursuits make no sense at all when faced with 20 to 30 years of "retirement" living. Society is struggling for a new term to describe this period of life because they have long sensed that the traditional concept is no longer relevant or valid.

How much longer then can the retirement savings industry continue to approach clients with the same plans and approaches? According to Jacqueline Quinn in the *Journal of Financial Planning,* "Because it is inevitable that the vision of retirement will continue to undergo a metamorphosis, some would argue that it behooves today's planners to adopt an entirely fresh approach to retirement planning, to reinvent retirement planning itself. Out are the old parameters of solely planning for a client's retirement, bearing in mind life expectancy increases. It is a much broader picture of retirement planning, the dimensions of which not only encompass the finances of retirement but the dimensions of the client's lifestyle (with its myriad nonfinancial issues). Planners are now helping clients plan not only for retirement, but how they are going to live in retirement."

## Financing the Rewired Life

If your retirement planning process is simply about "having X dollars at X age," you are doing nothing more than hammering horseshoes at the anvil. That hackneyed conversation does nothing more than prepare clients for the "artificial finish line." Life does not end or begin at age 62. Many clients are working in careers other than that which they desire with the hope that they can put away enough money to "do what they want" at age 62. These people must believe that life can begin at age 62. Others are preparing only in fiscal terms for retirement from their work at age 62 and are making no preparations for their time, knowledge, and energies past that point. These people are grossly underprepared for life past the age of 62. The retirement planning process can and must adapt to this new reality: *there is a lot of life left to live for today's "rewiree."* Let's begin using processes and services that better attend to this reality.

Michael Stein, author of *The Prosperous Retirement,* suggests that it's a time in life where an individual shifts from earning a living for the sake of economics to contributing to society with the goal of self-realization in mind." Retirement for baby boomers will become a classic animation of Maslow's Hierarchy of Needs as people move their minds and money up the pyramid toward self-actualization. Tomorrow's planners will find themselves engaging in conversation with two types of self-aware clients:

1. Those who want meaning and balance in their life, and can afford to resign from their paychecks.
2. Those who want meaning and balance in their life, but cannot afford to resign from their paychecks.

Just because those in the first category can afford to fully retire does not mean that they *should* fully retire if they are interested in pursuing meaning and achieving balance with their life. For many people who have the means to retire, part-time engagement in work that challenges and energizes them will be the key to their happy retirement period. Those who cannot afford retirement will need help exploring a work/life situation that will help them find the expression of meaning and attainment of balance they desire, while allowing the necessary income for the lifestyle they desire.

The conversation clearly needs to move from "how much money our clients will need to reach an artificial finish line" to "the kind of life they hope to live once they move past that line." Even better is a conversation that helps clients completely remove the artificial finish line and start work on transitioning to a life that does work and helps them pursue interests they love—at a pace they can live with.

Tomorrow's entrant to the retirement road will have little interest in being "finished." They instead will view it as a starting point.

For the conversation to move past a "pot-of-gold" artificial finish line, clients must be made aware of the differences between yesterday's retirement model and today's. The conversation between the advisor and client needs to move toward the realm of self-actualization, which is how the majority of prospective retirees are beginning to view the period of retirement—a time to self-actualize. This redefinition of retirement as a time for self-actualization is not restricted to the 60-plus crowd. Self-actualization seems to be the driving force behind the boomers—and the hub for the career choices of the gen-X population.

The redefinition of retirement raises a number of issues for you and your client to have a dialogue about. Consider the following:

- The. trend has been established for retirees to live long and active lives. How long should we plan on your living? How active do you want to be, and what costs are attached to those activities?
- Many people are extending their retirements into many phases—reeducation, entrepreneurial pursuits, charitable giving, adventure trips, and so on. What phases do you foresee for yourself, and what financial arrangements will be necessary to make these phases possible?
- Do you see the cost of your retirement lifestyle being the same as, less than, or more than what it is today? What adjustments need to be made?
- Will part-time work be one of your income sources in your retirement years?
- To accomplish your goals in your retirement years you will need tax and estate planning and insurance to protect your plans. Are you aware of how to utilize these various services?

Ross Levin, CFP, of Accredited Investors Inc. in Edina, Minnesota, tells a retirement transition story that fits quite well with the model of self-actualization as the target, rather than just a set amount of money at a certain age. He tells of a 53-year-old client who sold his business but had concerns about his investment assets supporting his lifestyle. Rather than going back to work in the same industry, Ross's dialogue with this client led to this man's taking a position in the public service sector, which was something he had always wanted to do. Despite the cut in salary, he is "in the black"—both at the income and self-actualization levels. How many advisors (when faced with this scenario) would have simply told the man the number of years he would have to work to reach his retirement?

The client referenced above is entering phase one of what may be a 40-year retirement journey. It is vital that he work with an advisor who understands this model of retirement living and offers as many options for self-actualizing as possible. The goal is more than monetary. Tomorrow's clients will measure their progress as much by what they contribute as by what they keep.

It is important for advisors who want to stay in step with the times to allow clients to offer their own definition of retirement. If you look up the word *retire* in the dictionary, you will see that it means to "withdraw." Suffice it to say that today's retirees are not the withdrawing type. They aim to squeeze everything they can out of life, to take the "tired" out of "retired." In the late 1960s, labor economist Seymour Wolfbein wrote that people of the baby boom generation would have at least five distinct careers—not jobs, but careers. Wolfbein prognosticated a time of retraining and reinvention and placed no upper limit when and where that training would end. It would seem that Wolfbein's crystal ball was crystal-clear regarding the "rewiring" boom ahead. The years previously set aside for reclining will now be used for redefining.

Consider the popular Silicon Valley myth that all the Internet start-ups were the product of 22-year-old Stanford Business School students. Ilan Greenberg wrote, "The pervasive image is of a start-up founder straight out of business school or still living in a college dorm. Only nine percent of those who have founded Internet firms are 29 or younger. People in their 40s and 50s make up nearly half of all start-up founders." Add to this the founders who were over 60, and the percentage of founders aged 40 to 60+ goes to 58 percent. Gray hair equals gray matter; make no mistake about it!

*As much as this generation of baby boomers demands challenges, they crave balance in their life between work and relationships.* It is the convergence of self-actualization and the realization of what truly makes for happiness that has forced the razing of traditional retirement models and redefining this phase of life on a more personal level. Advisors who understand this and begin the redefinition dialogue with their clients will find themselves connecting with clients in a new and dynamic manner.

It looks like it's time to leave the anvil behind and begin studying the quantum mechanics of the so-called "retirement" engine that will drive this society for the next 30 years.

## ReSOULution

Treat the retirement phase as a portal into a life of balance, freedom, and possible self-actualization. Instead of a finish line, treat it as a launching pad for a life of experimentation, applied wisdom, and fulfillment. It is a time to pursue purpose and the things that really matter to the soul. Make this visceral connection before attempting to connect dollar amounts to your client's retirement.

14

# What Do Your Clients Want Their Money to Do?

*The amassing of wealth is one of the worst species of idolatry—no idol is more debasing than the worship of money. To continue much longer overwhelmed by business cares and with most of my thoughts wholly upon the way to make more money in the shortest time must degrade me beyond the hope of permanent recovery.*

—Andrew Carnegie

As the *Mayflower* was carrying Pilgrims to liberty in America, another ship was simultaneously sent to transport a load of slaves to these seekers of liberty. They dedicated their lives to finding freedom and used their resources to perpetuate bondage. It was this conflict of interest that eventually brought this new nation to a state of implosion. These two ships are a fitting metaphor for your clients' lives as they pursue wealth and liberty but simultaneously entangle themselves in the process.

As the most prosperous people on earth, we need to pause and ask ourselves if we are we earning the appropriate dividends of life satisfaction on that wealth. Has Madison Avenue convinced us that we will never have enough to be truly happy, that true wealth is always the next rung on the ladder?

Our money has the power to either liberate us or create more bondage. It has the power to help us find significance or to drive us further into despair, depending on how we appropriate it. Money can be utilized in a way that introduces a sense of balance into our lives or be invested in enterprises that do nothing but perpetuate and even accelerate the manic pace. Money can be used to create borders of security for our present and future or can be used in ways that up the ante on our daily anxiety level. Our attitude toward our money can be the difference between a state of contentment and a state of depression.

In 2002, for the first time in the history of the Nobel Prize, the prize for economics was given to a psychologist, Daniel Kahneman, whose work has uncovered the first of many layers of emotional and psychological conflict in our decision-making processes, including our relationships with money. As a culture, we continue to make the same monetary mistakes over and over, and the return we get is increased anxiety and dissatisfaction.

The study that revealed that the more money Americans make, the less sleep they get provokes us to ask, "Is this because wealth and opportunity has placed their minds in a state of heightened alertness or because it has opened the floodgates of anxiety?" Many of you have seen, in your firsthand experience as advisors, that it is generally more of the latter. The great disconnect we have witnessed in our culture is between the pursuit of wealth and the distribution of that wealth in ways that increase one's sense of satisfaction. Again, we may be getting money, but we are not necessarily *getting our money's worth*.

## What's the Money For?

Consider the degrees of frustration that many are experiencing as a result of their money:

- A couple, already under considerable financial stress, goes out and doubles the size of their mortgage when receiving a slight pay raise. One of them works for a firm that has been hit hard by the economic downturn.
- A woman frets over her mortgage for years. Her accountant tells her she needs the mortgage for a tax deduction every time she brings up the topic. She follows his advice even though it leads to sleepless nights. She is 81 years old.
- A man who is making great money and whose career is flourishing can't bring himself to enjoy any of his money because he's controlled by a mortal fear of being poor.

- A woman feels her skills and gifts are being wasted by not utilizing them in her career. She has so much debt, however, that she doesn't feel she can afford to change career paths.
- Both a husband and his wife feel trapped in their all-consuming careers working with people they wish they didn't have to work with because they are afraid to make a change and don't really know the options available to them.
- A man receiving a large bonus places it all in a risky stock bet in biotech. He watches it disappear within a year because he can't force himself to sell it and acknowledge his mistake.
- A woman uses money from a divorce settlement to purchase an expensive foreign vehicle, a high-priced European vacation, and comes home to face rising levels of financial anxiety because of her decisions.
- A couple in their 60s move all their money out of safe havens when the market is booming because they don't want to miss out on high returns and then reverse courses as the market hits bottom out of fear of losing everything.

All of us could be reaping much greater dividends from the money we have than we are currently experiencing; a weighing of the emotional consequences of financial decisions would cause us all to take more prudent paths with how we earn, how we invest, and how we utilize our money. By weighting our financial decisions with emotional as well as material rationale, we increase the possibility of getting our money's worth in terms of happiness, balance, security, and meaning, the four great intangible cornerstones of life (more on these shortly).

Your clients know, but do not align themselves with, the knowledge that their money should not be used in a way that works against satisfaction, security, balance, and happiness. Yet it is. Millions utilize their money in ways that lead to greater increased anxiety rather than prosperity and peace of mind. Your opportunity is to educate your clients to ensure that they see the big picture.

## Settle the Big Picture

If we all took a closer look at the manners in which we appropriate the money we receive we could find adjustments (some small, some significant) that would immediately produce a dividend of less anxiety, greater security and increased satisfaction. For this to happen, money must be placed in its proper context. Asking your clients to answer the following question is a first step: *Is money a means or an end for you?*

If your client's answer is that it is an end—that he just wants a big pile of money at the end of the race—then this client might not be the most enjoyable relationship for you. If his money is a means to something more important in his life—a tool for moving him toward greater security, happiness, and balance—then this question will help to guide both an internal dialogue and some decision-making processes designed to set that client free from financial anxiety, and possibly help to increase the intangible benefits from the paychecks he is collecting.

## The Four Cornerstones of Life

If you ask people what they want from their money and their lives, the answers you hear repeatedly are *happiness, balance, security,* and *meaning.* How well and how wisely we manage our money has an impact on all four of these cornerstones of life. In fact, it is quite easy, by making poor financial decisions to compromise our happiness, security, balance in life, and even our sense of meaning if we are enslaved to money-producing activities that keep us from doing the things that make us feel a sense of purpose. Following are descriptions of these four cornerstones and their relationship to your client's money.

### Happiness: Wanting What You Already Have

> *Money won't make you happy, but neither will poverty.*
>
> —Anonymous

Madison Avenue is keenly interested in helping us to develop our peripheral vision regarding the homes and possessions of our neighbors. Advertisers are interested in feeding discontentment. Create a void and fill that void with a product is how the thinking goes. "*This* will make you happy" is how the ad copy reads.

But people eventually learn, or at least we hope they learn, that this brand of consumerism will only increase their hunger and discontentment.

Author/theologian G. K. Chesterton said there are only two ways to get enough. One is to continually strive for more and more, and the other is to be content with less than you already have.

Warren Buffett said the only two things that really make you happy are good health and people who love you, and you can't buy either one of those. That being said, it still stands to reason that many people have bought themselves unhappiness with money decisions they have made, and if that is possible, it is possible to raise our level of happiness by making some wiser decisions with our money.

### Balance: Walking the Tightrope between Too Much and Not Enough

When we can manage to get work, family, leisure, and personal development in balance, we truly start enjoying life. Balance in life is an investment issue, namely, how well we invest our *time*. Achieving balance is a perpetual balancing act, not a "one and done" decision.

Many in our society feel they are investing far too much time in work and far too little in family or leisure or personal development. Often, this is the case because of the way they have managed their resources. They are forced to work long hours and extra jobs to pay for stuff. Relationships suffer. Life satisfaction suffers. Destinies suffer. *Their schedules have become enslaved to their debt schedules.*

Money can be utilized in such a way that it actually restores balance to our lives. Those who have done so have learned to readjust and use their resources in such a way that it restores a sense of balance and personal fulfillment to their lives. Their life is no longer about making money. Their money is about making a life.

### Security: Doing What You Want with Your Tomorrow

Security may be the greatest intangible benefit properly managed money can deliver to our lives. If I do things right and invest the right amount of resources in both the present and future, I can go to sleep at night with the assurance that tomorrow "belongs to me." My time is mine to invest any way I choose.

Once we forfeit or lose that security, we live with fear: fear of losing our job, fear of never being able to pursue our dreams, fear of not having enough in retirement years. This probably sounds like a lot of your clients.

Each time we make a financial decision, we are adding to or subtracting from a sense of security. Every person is different in regards to how much they need and where they need to put those resources to feel secure. It is important to listen to these feelings when offering financial advice. From your client's point of view, you need to ask, "What is the point of following the advice of some professional if it causes you to not be able to sleep at night?"

### Significance: Making the Best Possible Use of Our Time, Abilities, and Passions

Viktor Frankl stated that man's primary motivation was the need to find significance and meaning in his life. People are motivated by a need to somehow make a difference in others' lives—to feel they are making a contribution that is significant or has meaning.

As a result of financial pressures, many people have unplugged themselves from the activities and pursuits that fulfill this sense of meaning. In quiet moments of desperation, they ask themselves, "What is the significance of all this?" Many are caught up in "activity traps" where there is much sound and show but little meaning.

Many people, however, by starting with the way they manage their finances, have been able to move their lives toward a place where their hands, head, and heart are working together in activities that fulfill this inescapable need for meaning and significance, and sometimes in a fashion that is unpredictable and unconventional.

Hal told me how he had spent 20 years as a social worker and counselor and had burned out. Through his years of experience, however, he had noted that many people's problems were rooted in and stemmed from money management issues. Hal became a financial advisor and told me, "It sounds strange to some, but I have a much greater feeling of meaning and significance in what I'm doing now because I feel like if I can help people do the right things financially, I can help to save them much misery and add to their life satisfaction in immeasurable ways. It's not that what I was doing before wasn't significant, it is that what I'm doing now is more meaningful to *me*."

It may be a career step or it may be a directional shift, but, either way, financial implications are involved in the move that puts the "me" in meaning in life. Your challenge is to help your clients find that.

## Finding the Keys

Harry Houdini had never failed an escape challenge, save one. One day Houdini walked into a jail cell and the door clanged shut behind him. From under his belt Houdini removed a strong and flexible piece of metal. He began to work; something seemed odd about this particular lock. He worked for 30 minutes with no results. Frustrated, he labored for another hour and a half. By now he was soaked in sweat and completely exasperated at his inability to pick this lock. Drained from the experience, Harry Houdini collapsed in frustration and failure and fell against the door. To his surprise and embarrassment, the door swung open— it had never been locked! The door was locked only in the mind of Houdini.

We know that it is possible to have prosperity and peace of mind. We have seen clients who manage their lives and resources in wise counsel and careful protection of life quality. These people are those who realize that there are both fiscal and philosophical keys for approaching financial and life decisions that are as good for the soul as they are for the portfolio. Chances are that these individuals are working with a financial advisor who possesses a similar sagacity. If they are not, they are certainly looking for one.

After interviewing many such settled individuals, I developed the following list of *fiscalophical* keys that open up emotional space in our lives and provide more peace of mind.

### Fiscalophical Key Number One

Help your clients decide what they want from their money and life by asking them these important philosophical questions:

- Is your life about making money, or is your money about making a life?
- What do you want to be when you grow up?
- How much is your paycheck costing you?
- If you had all the money you would ever need right now, what would you do differently?

### Fiscalophical Key Number Two

Help your clients remove the clutter from their money memory by having them:

- Examine the roots of their money behavior.
- Look at lessons they learned about money when they were young.

- Take an honest assessment of their worst money fears.
- Balance the books on money mistakes they've made in the past.

### Fiscalophical Key Number Three

Help your clients move their money from the fantasy fund to the reality rollover by settling their emotional/investment ledgers between best intentions and denied reality:

- Recover from market hangovers.
- Admit past errors and move past them.
- Stop blaming others for traps created by their own greed.
- Admit that they've often followed the insane herd for fear of getting left behind.
- Realize valuable lessons about denial they can easily fall into regarding their own financial behavior.

### Fiscalophical Key Number Four

Realize that the bottom line is not a number; it's quality of life, not just quantity of accounts:

- Understand the tether that connects your client's money and life.
- What is the value your client is willing to place, and what is she willing to pay for security, peace of mind, and anxiety-free living?
- Make money a servant, not a god.

Many people live their entire lives allowing money to dictate every move, turn, and life-changing circumstance. The end result for those people is stress, frustration, loneliness, and dissatisfaction with what they have gained. Ask those who have allowed money to exclusively dictate their working lives and their decisions regarding retirement whether they might not later regret not making better use of their most valuable resource—time. We have a world of people who are hungry to learn how to use their money to create quality in their lives and the lives of others. The right relationship with the right kind of financial advisor, one who really gets it, can have a virtual Houdini effect in their life. The doors will swing open toward getting what they always hoped their money would deliver. Seize the opportunity to make a true difference in your clients' lives.

## ReSOULution

Help each of your clients move their thinking from clutter to clarity regarding what they want their money to do. Bridging the gap between means and meaning is the result of helping people clarify exactly what life benefits they hope to reap from their financial harvest.

# PART III

# DIALOGUE RESOULUTIONS

Over the past few years I have kept my ear peeled to conversations that are critical to life but that seem to be lacking in financial services. These observations led me to the chapters in this section, covering an array of topics that may or will affect our lives at critical junctures, including the possibility of disability, the denial of the inevitable (death), the rearrangement of retirement and its impact on your clients' lives, and how your clients can give in a meaningful way of the assets (material and nonmaterial) that they gather in their lifetime. If you are not engaging at some point with the following dialogues, I encourage you to start making room for them in your conversations.

# CHAPTER 15

# The History Dialogue

## FINDING YOUR CLIENTS' FUTURE IN THEIR PAST

*. . . What's past is prologue. . . .*

—William Shakespeare

On a flight to Phoenix, I noticed that the man next to me was reading a book that I had just completed. A conversation ensued wherein this man revealed that he was the CEO of a billion-dollar, publicly traded manufacturing firm. I began to inquire into his background and the journey that resulted in his current station in life. Eventually, this gentleman, blushing because he had been talking about his life and business for over 30 minutes, said to me, "I'm sorry to just talk about myself—what is it that you do?"

I told him that my profession may sound unusual to him and that what I did was "think up questions about money."

He said, "That *is* unusual. Go ahead and ask me one now," so I asked this man the question, "What is your first money-related memory?" His eyes seemed to glaze over and his voice sounded like it went monotone as he remarked, "I am sitting on a couch in Cleveland, and the couch is sitting on the street corner. We have been evicted from our home for the third time. My father washes windows for a living—works 12 to 14 hours a day and cannot support his 11 children. Neighbors are driving by and gawking at us at we sit on the couch."

It was a stunning and remarkable answer. Many clients will not have such a dramatic response, at which point you can say, "Often, no recollection comes to mind right away but surfaces later. If and when you think of something, tell me about it. The stories usually are significant, which is why they are preserved in our memory bank."

I asked this executive if he had a financial planner. He said that he did as a part of an executive benefits program. I then inquired as to whether or not this financial planner had ever heard this story about his childhood. The man replied, "No, I've never told him. But then again, he's never asked."

I often tell this story to financial advisors when I am conducting trainings on client discovery. After I tell the story, I ask two questions, one of which is a trap.

Question 1: If this gentleman were your client, how many of you would want to know this story for the sake of context and understanding?

The answer is always an overwhelming affirmative, "Yes, we would both want and *need* to know this story," and then these advisors go on to comment on the reasons they would want and need to know the story:

- This experience would probably inform us of his risk tolerance.
- He probably maintains a certain amount of fear of poverty, in spite of his wealth.
- He might fear that his children will suffer the same sort of humiliation due to lack of money.

At this point I ask the trick question (Question 2): "How are you going to hear this profound and pivotal story without asking the question I just asked?"

The first time I told this story in an advisor training session, one of the advisors present asked me, "What is your first recollection around money?" I let my memory bank go to work, and in just a few seconds I saw an image of the ice cream vendor riding his bicycle-driven freezer into our neighborhood as a young child. As he announced himself by ringing a bell, chills went up and down our spines as we thought about the chill about to hit our throats.

We would scatter and race home if we didn't have a dime in our pocket to gather the needed coin before the ice cream vendor disappeared.

On one particular day, I ran into the house in a panic and asked my father, "Dad, can I have a dime, please!?! The ice cream guy is here and he'll be leaving!"

My father held out a dime, but as I went to grab it he held on, furthering my flustered state, and said, "Son, go ahead and buy one if you want, but I've got to tell you that if you jump on your bike and ride over to Boyer's grocery you can get the same one for seven cents and have enough left over for three jawbreakers or pieces of bubble gum."

Now he was speaking my language.

I ran outside, jumped on my bike, and rode just a few short blocks to the neighborhood store and came back with the push-up *and* the jawbreakers and tormented my friends throughout the afternoon with my bonus prize. When they asked how I got the jawbreakers, I told them of my shopping genius like it was my own idea.

The advisor who asked me for this story then asked me, "And what lesson, if any, do you think you've carried forward from that early experience?"

I hadn't thought about that up to this point. However, I had an epiphany right then and there: This was probably the experience that had cast the mold on my insistence that, if you look around or negotiate, there is always a better bargain to be found. I also thought of how my brother was the exact same way (maybe even more so) with every negotiation.

I now understood something about myself that I had not known five minutes before. The student had taught his teacher well. My story was not as dramatic as the one told to me by the gentleman on the plane, but it is/was still significant.

And therein lies the rub. This type of significant story will not automatically surface by asking the sort of questions advisors ask on the average "fact–finding" or discovery forms commonly used in this industry. This leads me to the next topic: the industry's view on what constitutes "discovery." The industry is notoriously left-brained in what it deems to be an acceptable discovery form. The very term *fact finder* indicates all we need to know about the breadth of thought and insight these forms are seeking.

## Just the Facts

I often make the joke that, based on viewing scores of firms' discovery forms, we could save a lot of paper and time if the major intent of the form were reduced to the following:

- What is your address?
- How much do you have?

One of the consulting projects I'm often asked to undertake is the grading of discovery tools on the basis of balance between right- and left-brain inquiry, qualitative and quantitative, content and context, means and meaning. Most firms' forms end up at a D or a C at best, with the occasional exception. I recently graded a Canadian bank's discovery profile with a B+ because they succeeded in aligning their questions in the proper order and in achieving a rare balance between the quantitative and qualitative.

Most people absolutely dread filling out left-brain sides of questionnaires. (My wife and I have squabbles and contests to settle who gets stuck with the task.) The left-brain side of these inquiries is like a Bataan Death March of numbers and facts, whereas the right-brain side of these inquiries can be enjoyable and thought provoking.

## Discovery Forms and Forms of Discovery

I once had a top firm call to get my feedback on their "new and improved" discovery form that they were about to roll out to their advisors. "Much more comprehensive" was the description they gave it. They sent it to me on a Friday and arranged for a conference call on Monday to discuss the piece. I was excited to see the piece, based on their enthusiasm for it, but was completely deflated by what I saw. There's nothing more disappointing than dealing with people who don't really get it but are convinced that they do.

Their "new and improved" discovery form had a total of 100 questions that needed to be answered. A total of five were qualitative in nature. And if the skewing toward numbers and statistical inquiry were not bad enough, the leading qualitative question read, "Which of the following five is your goal?," followed by five company-provided selected choices for your life goals.

Our conference call came on Monday. Their crew was assembled and excitedly asked, "What did you think of the new form?" Wondering what in the world the old form had looked like if this were the better, enhanced version, I offered, "I don't know if I should congratulate the form's architects or your marketing research team that was able—in question number 95—to boil all a client's goals down to five choices." I then proceeded to offer the critique they didn't really want to hear. They thought they understood but really didn't. You can gather every number and fact that pertains to a client's life, including assets, but those numbers do not help you *know your client*.

When we set about putting together the financial jigsaw that clients lay on the table before us, the first corner piece we must gather is the personal history of the client. This history piece contains within it the emotional context of why this individual comes to the planner in the first place. Many planners—for qualitative purposes—move quickly to the goals discussion when, in fact, the goals discussion is two stages premature. Before you discuss *Where do you want to be?* (goals), you would benefit from the foundational insights of *Where are you now?* (transitions) and *Where have you been?* (history). You need to know where you're clients are now, and where they've been, before you can help them get to where they want to be.

## The Advisor as Biographer

There is much that can be learned by acting as a biographer for your clients. You can gain a much deeper understanding of your clients by inquiring into their background, culture, socioeconomic experience, values, and formative experiences. Each client (and his or her mate) has a unique story to tell and a very personal perspective regarding money. Following are four fundamental "history" inquiries that have a bearing on your planning work. Bear in mind as you read these inquiries that discovery is an ongoing and dynamic process and that you don't need to learn the answers to all these questions in the first meeting with a client, although the sooner you gain the knowledge the better—and sooner—you'll be able to help your client achieve her goals.

### Their Journey

*"Where are you from?"*

*"What was it like growing up?"*

*"What did your parents do?"*

*"How did you get from there to here?"*

*"How did you meet the most important people in your life?"*

*"How did you end up doing what you are doing today?"*

The answers to these questions reveal the cultural and familial DNA that may have played an important role in shaping your clients' values, setting their expectations for life, establishing their socioeconomic goals and comfort levels, and defining their perspectives.

### Formative Experiences with Money

*"What lessons were you taught about money as a child?"*

*"What is your first memory or recollection around money?"*

*"What was your first opportunity to make and manage your own money?"*

The answers you hear in this inquiry are both practical and philosophical but imperative in terms of reading the financial blueprint that guides this client in financial matters and the scripts that control their feelings and comfort levels in financial decisions.

### Lessons Learned

*"What are the best and/or worst experiences you have had with money or investing?"*

*"Who have been your chief sources of information/advice when making financial decisions?"*

"Burned once, your fault; burned twice, my fault" is how the universal code for stupid decision making goes. Given the opportunity to talk about their best and worst decisions and the information sources that led to them might just end up being both a beneficial exercise in self-awareness for your clients and an obvious piece of due diligence for you.

### Experiences within the Financial Services Industry

*"Have you had any experiences with other financial services providers, good or bad, that you think would be worth your time to tell me about?'*

Financial liberty is needed for the "huddled masses." Because of integrity issues previously discussed, there are a lot of "walking wounded" in the financial services marketplace. Many clients and prospects could be diagnosed with PTSS (post-traumatic sales syndrome) and are paralyzed at worst and distrusting at best. Why not pull the source of financial fears and distrust to the top of the table ASAP and help your client get some perspective on the matter and gain enough confidence in you to move forward with needed financial decisions.

If they have had a great experience, you'll now be aware of the exact standard you must keep. But, chances are, if they'd had a great experience, they wouldn't be shopping for a new advisor.

## A Professional Approach

Critics of my theories on financial life planning used to claim that asking such probing questions bordered on practicing psychology. I respectfully disagreed at the time and firms have now seen enough return in tangible results in response to these inquires that it is no longer a matter of debate.

I have always maintained that asking about a client's history, especially those aspects of history that are germane to the task the provider performs is a mark of professionalism (i.e., the doctor who inquires about a patient's health history versus the doctor who fails to do so). The person who inquires into the past is doing appropriate due diligence, not practicing psychology.

It is only when a provider begins to attempt therapeutic interpretation that this line between dialogue and psychology is crossed. With just a few simple questions, good advisors can help their clients discover why they respond as they do to money issues and maybe even why or how they might be sabotaging their relationship with a financial advisor, family member, and so on.

Is this discovery work psychological in nature? Of course it is, but so is measuring a client's risk tolerance, and all good planners do that. Money is an emotionally laden topic for people. So the question arises, "How do I practice financial advice effectively and ignore historical issues that clients have with their money?" You don't: any professional provider who ignores his client's history does so at his own risk.

My sister suffers from a mental illness that requires her to live in a halfway house–type institution. Recently, this institution began an effort to help some of its residents move out and live independently in apartments in the vicinity of the halfway house. Social workers were raising my sister's hopes (and diminishing her sense of contentment) with these visions of emancipation.

My mother paid a visit to both the social worker and the doctor to see how much of her history they were aware of. The major reason she had to be institutionalized 12 years previous was that, on three separate occasions, she had accidentally started fires in her apartment. When my mother talked to the doctor and social worker, she discovered they were basing their recommendations solely on current observations—neither of them knew anything of her history of starting fires. You can see how important your client's history can be, not only to your client, but to you as well.

## Buried Clues

The past holds many clues to the present and to the future for our clients. In the stories from yesteryear, we find the source of patterns with money—permanent reference points for their approach to money management and experiences that drive their behavior. The successful financial life planner seeks to form such a partnership with his clients. The lifeblood of that partnership is understanding—the sort of understanding that breeds empathy and appreciation for your clients' journeys: their joys and sorrows, the lessons they have borrowed from life, and the type of people they want to associate with in money management. Any good doctor would never treat a patient without knowing and understanding her medical history. If our goal as financial planners is to improve our client's fiscal health, we need to understand fiscal history.

I would prefer to have a client's accounting of their experiences before I would know their account balances. Stories reveal what numbers cannot. A well-constructed "what's your history?" dialogue will answer important contextual questions between you and your client:

- What circumstances shaped this client's views and values?
- What money experiences formed the "scripts" that control this client's money behaviors?
- What financial decisions have made the most indelible marks upon this client's psyche?

- Who are the players that drive the decisions this client makes?
- What are this client's expectations and fears of working with a financial professional?

I once heard an accountant talk about how he believed that every number on a W-2 tax form had a story behind it and that learning these stories was what made his job most interesting. I heard another advisor say that the greatest risk a financial professional takes is in *not* asking these questions and in not knowing these formative stories. Once these stories are told and heard, your client moves to a place of greater appreciation for you and your interest level, and to a place where empathy has been brought out in Technicolor in the unique story of his life.

Why take the risk of some competitor's being the first to discover these stories? Look past the numbers and, with an archeologist's zeal and a biographer's curiosity, discover the stories that created these numbers.

### ReSOULution

Raise the standard of empathy in your life and business. Do not be satisfied with superfluous knowledge of people and with chit-chat instead of dialogue. Demonstrate through the quality of your questions the ethos that every human being is irreplaceably important and worth knowing.

# CHAPTER 16

## Goals Are Overrated

*Take no thought for tomorrow. Sufficient for today is the evil thereof.*

—Matt: 6:34

*Connect with clients on "what will be" not just on "what might be."*
—Mitch Anthony

Focus on your client's goals." "Find out where they want to be." "Help them achieve their dreams." Such phrases have become half-mantra/half cliché in the modern advisory world. And if you're smart, you'll build your client conversations around something other than pie in the sky.

The fragile, the fickle and frivolous, whimsical musings, and capricious contexts are no place to build the foundation for a lifetime advisory relationship. There is a place for a goals conversation, but it isn't in the formative stage of the relationship. A better place than goals to commence a relationship that will last is in the realm of transitions, changes, passages, and concerns on the road of life.

It's a matter of focusing on the things that *are* happening, not just the things that we *want* to happen. It has been said that "if you want to make God laugh, tell Him your plans." Life is what happens while we are making our plans. Do you want to anchor your relationships on the events that will happen or on those that might happen? Better think about it because your answer today will determine whether you exist on a foundation of rock or sand 10 years from now.

Most financial services firms have made the mistake of trying to get concrete on a goals discussion too early in the game. There is a definite time and place for the goals and vision of life discussion, but I suggest that it is after you have settled the more concrete issues facing your clients. After you have assisted clients in the "what is and will be" categories, it is then a good time to assist them in bringing their visions to life.

Connect on the basis of the inevitable, not just that of wishful thinking—the truth is, a lot of your clients' goals are not going to ever happen because life is going to get in the way. Parents are going to age and need assistance, restricting your clients logistically and financially. There are going to be health challenges. Children are going to grow up, move on, move back, and continue to bring challenges into your clients' lives. Companies are going to "change directions," pensions are going to get halved, entire professions are going to become "automated." The best-laid investment plans as well as the markets are not obliged to go along with your clients' goals and hopes. The only thing that is certain in life is that life will certainly change. And while life is changing direction, it is not necessarily taking its cues from us or our clients.

We would be much better off asking our clients what their concerns are, what passages of life they are going through, or what changes they see coming than we are spouting the banal and overused, "Tell me about your goals." Ever seen the deer in the headlights response to that question? The truth is that a lot of people don't know yet what their goals are: they are too busy dealing with the present to concern themselves with the future.

## What Was I Thinking?

One day while rummaging through old files, I came across a "goals sheet" that I had been cajoled into filling out in a workshop. I remember being given the dire directive at the time about the absolute necessity of (1) writing down your goals, and (2) keeping these goals in front of you. I don't remember the exact statistics the instructor gave, but the odds were somewhere between the penthouse and the outhouse if you failed to subscribe to these commandments. So I wrote all my goals down and promptly misplaced the goals sheet, not to be seen again until five years later. After reading it, I was actually relieved that I had lost it!

Why? In retrospect, my goals fell into two neat categories: (1) already happened (even without ever looking at them again), and, (2) what was I smoking at the time? (How could I have ever convinced myself that I wanted *that* to happen?) I guess if a goal is really a goal it will take root organically. Plus, if it's not a goal, and is instead a whim or capricious desire, then the winds of personal awareness will blow it away to some other garden. Many of our so-called goals change as often as the fashion world. I think of this every time I hear a former boat owner quip, "The two best days in a boat owner's life are the day you buy it and the day you sell it."

## Come Back from the Future

I just happen to feel that, for advisors intent on building serious lifetime relationships, conversations about goals and dreams are not the place to start. They are too fuzzy, too elusive, and too susceptible to impulse and fad to suffice as the foundational dialogue in a *clients-for-life* type of relationship. Instead, first build that foundation on the present and immediate future in terms of realities, concerns, and transitions of everyday life. Once these inevitable events are planned for, you can move on to the desired and hoped for.

For the past few years the Financial Life Planning (FLP) Institute has been researching both life transitions and life goals and their impact on financial well-being. The Institute differentiates transitions and goals this way: *Goals are what people want to happen. Transitions are what is happening.* You are much better off getting in touch and staying in touch with your clients' transitions first as those issues that have the greatest impact on their financial status and health.

The FLP Institute research has uncovered 65 life transitions that take place between cradle and grave. These transitions fall into four categories:

1. Personal/family transitions
2. Career/work transitions
3. Financial/investment transitions
4. Community/legacy transitions

We have also developed a checklist that you can give to clients to check off, thereby indicating which matters and changes in life they are faced with or most concerned about.

The Institute provides comprehensive research on each life transition that enables the advisor to take a mini-course regarding the general considerations, discovery questions, financial implications, and educational resources around each of the 65 life transitions. Once the client has indicated what their chief concerns are, you are now able to engage them in a meaningful conversation about what they need to think about to navigate successfully through this change in life. This conversation is centered on the here and now and the coming-soon aspects of their life, and has built within it the urgency to act because quality of life is on the line—for themselves and for those they love.

Recently, the FLP Institute completed a national survey on the top 10 life concerns of advisory clients. It is ironic to note that many of these concerns are rarely mentioned in the typical advisor/client conversation nor in the typical firm's literature. A classic example of this is the number one response, "Concern about an aging parent," which was far and away the top concern but is scarcely surveyed by the typical advisor. Other concerns and transitions that made the top 10 list include "reevaluating my investment philosophy" (people are looking to anchor their plans in sound principles and stable investment philosophy), concern about personal health, and developing an estate plan (see Table 16.1).

**Table 16.1   Top 10 FLP Survey Results: Transitions**

| Rank | Life Transition |
| --- | --- |
| 1 | Concerned about an aging parent |
| 2 | Reconsidering investment philosophy |
| 3 | Concerned about personal health |
| 4 | Develop or review an estate plan |
| 5 | Concerned about debt |
| 6 | Give to church/religious organizations or causes |
| 7 | Providing assistance to a family member |
| 8 | Develop an end-of-life plan |
| 9 | Phasing into retirement |
| 10 | Concerned about the health of spouse or child |

In looking at most firms' literature, you would assume there are only three transitions in life (college, retirement, and death) rather than 65. Could it be that the industry lacks the education to engage in meaningful conversation about the other aspects of life and/or lacks the imagination to see how its products and services could be utilized to meet the needs of these transitions? I suspect it is both.

A director of training for one of the biggest firms in the financial services industry made a pithy observation on this dearth of "real life" advice regarding a recent life transition he and his wife passed through—their daughter's wedding. He said, "We just experienced the biggest financial distribution we will probably ever experience, and we were in no way, shape, or form prepared for the impact. Not only did we see our investible assets take a major hit, but our plans for the future are profoundly impacted as well. This is a conversation we wish we'd had ahead of time."

The here and now and the near horizon: that's where to focus your primary attention. On real life as it unfolds before your clients' eyes. There is plenty of opportunity right in front of you.

## Five Years from Today

My friend Gary recently called me after experiencing a first-time meeting with a financial advisor from an insurance company. Gary had scheduled the appointment because he had some risk management issues he was concerned about. He said that this advisor made the ceremonial chit-chat about family and hobbies and then turned the conversation to business with the lead-in, "So tell me, Gary, where do you see yourself five years from today?"

Gary commented to me regarding this ubiquitous and banal question, "Every emotional cell in my being shut down. I mean that question is so artificial, so contrived, and I just knew it was right out of the training manual."

Gary politely ended the meeting.

Gary, who is in his early 50s, finished his story with this epilogue, "This guy wants to come in here and talk to me about pie in the sky, but I've got some real life issues right in front of my nose, the first of which is not losing what has taken me over 30 years to build. I'm much more interested in protecting what I have than I am in accumulating at this point."

Why has the financial services industry tried to operate contrary to years of documented psychological research? Maslow, through his Hierarchy of Needs, discovered that people cannot and will not address higher-level emotional needs until the lower-level needs are first met. *Survival* is the most basic need of all. Once survival is insured, then a person is ready to move up the pyramid toward meeting *safety* needs, then helping those they love by addressing self-esteem issues, and finally this thing called *self-actualization,* closely correlated to goals.

Whether through ignorance, misguidance, or hubris, the financial services industry routinely trains its advisors to fly right past the first four levels in Maslow's hierarchy and encourages them to establish a relational premise on goals! What's the point? As the example with Gary illustrates so well, the advisor, by hop-scotching to the top of the pyramid and flying right past the important *safety* issue that was driving Gary's concerns, he missed an irretrievable opportunity for establishing a relationship.

Most of your clients are in need of a conversation that focuses on the first two steps of the pyramid: survival and safety. "Will I outlive my money?," "How do I protect the gains I've made?," "How can I help my parents or my children?," and so on.

## "Visioning" versus Goal Setting

One juncture in life that does lend itself rather well to a more goal-focused approach is the retirement stage. Rather than asking people to set concrete goals, it is more advantageous to give them the opportunity to "play with the possibilities" and to address their more general goals, such as "relax more," "pursue other interests," "seek personal growth," and so on.

One fund company, Van Kampen Funds, took this idea seriously in bringing my New RetireMentality concept out to the marketplace and created "vision cards" for advisors to use in their retirement discussions with clients. There are 12 cards with beautiful images of mountains, golf courses, walking shoes, books, and other images that indicate the more general goals tied to an emerging lifestyle. There are no words on these cards, so how they are interpreted is up to the client. The advisor lays the 12 cards out on the table and instructs the client to "pick out three of these cards that represent what you see your life in retirement being." After they pick their cards out, the advisor then asks the client to explain why they picked the cards they did. They are now gathering a vision story and associating their practice with that vision. Needless to say, this tool has proven to be enormously successful for the both Van Kampen and their advisor clients.

On the New RetireMentality web site, newretirementality.com, we provide a visioning exercise for the general public where they can print out their life vision with small pictures and descriptors on an 8½ × 11 page. Figure 16.1 shows the visioning questionnaire.

**Figure 16.1   The Visioning Questionnaire**

Whereas goal-setting jargon can often lead to constipated dialogue and a deer-in-the-headlights lack of articulation and commitment, visioning dialogues don't seem to suffer from the same pitfalls, as they are free form, general and strategic in direction and require no immediate and firm commitment of will and energy. Visioning is like choosing a life direction, but not the specific highway or vehicle yet.

I reiterate the point that visioning is useful in its time and its place but advise beginning in the here and now to anchor your position in your client's life.

"Take no thought for tomorrow. Sufficient for today is the evil thereof." These famous words from the Sermon on the Mount make for good guideposts for an effective inaugural and periodic, touch-point client dialogue. There is a time and place for a goals conversation. But the time is after all of today's concerns have been surfaced and addressed and these emotional scores are settled.

Dig deep enough into the here and now and you'll find no trouble making connections for the sweet by-and-by.

## ReSOULution

Help your clients get a grip on the here and now, producing confidence that they can manage their future. Actualization has its place, at the top of the emotional hierarchy, and is best addressed after foundational needs are answered. Attend to possibilities once the probabilities have been addressed.

# 17

# Funding "Single Moments"

*And in the end, it's not the years in your life that count. It's the life in your years.*

—Abraham Lincoln

My son Nate graduated with a degree in wildlife management and had just completed the law enforcement academy. I remember well the 10-year-old's glee in a grown man's eyes when he told me he had landed a job in Fairbanks, Alaska. "Alaska, Dad," he told me, "the last great American frontier and an outdoorsman's dream."

His new employer told him they wanted him to start in the first week of January, which meant that he would be required to traverse the great Alaskan highway on the week between Christmas and the New Year—a 56-hour drive in potentially treacherous conditions, pulling a trailer with all his worldly possessions in the dead of winter. As soon as he described the trip to me, I knew it was something we had to do together. It was a singular opportunity to help my oldest son launch his life that would never come again.

*Imagine a music lover sitting in the concert hall while the most noble measures of his favorite symphony resound in his ears. He feels that shiver of emotion which we experience in the presence of the purest beauty. Suppose now that at such a moment we should ask this person whether his life has meaning. He would have to reply that it had been worth living if only to experience this ecstatic moment. For even though only a single moment is in question, the greatness of a life can be measured by the greatness of a moment: the height of a mountain range is not given by the height of some valley, but by that of the tallest peak. In life, too, the peaks decide the meaningfulness of the life, and a single moment can retroactively flood an entire life with meaning.*

—Viktor Frankl, *The Doctor and the Soul*

## The Great Alaskan Highway Ride: Day One—Guns N' Roses

When I asked him if I could join him, I sensed both excitement and relief. Our first day would take us through Minnesota, North Dakota, and Manitoba. This trip would, in many ways, teach me about the large tapestry of life and the small pieces that make it beautiful. The first reminder came as our route took us through North Dakota and we drove right by the farming community where my mother had grown up.

My son has eclectic taste in music, and I would be well acquainted with the bluegrass of Dell McCurry and the rock of Guns N' Roses by the time we reached our destination. The latter group turned out to be an omen of what was to come at the Canadian border.

*"Momma lay these guns in the ground, I can't shoot them anymore."* Axl Rose "croons" like fingernails on a blackboard as we approach a one-hour inspection because of the guns we were carrying, including a 12-gauge shotgun, and .22 and .30-.30 caliber rifles.

I had never spent more than few minutes at a border crossing before, but this would be different. I guess when border guards see a pickup truck with a four-wheeler in the bed pulling a U-Haul with guns galore inside they are on red alert, not to mention the fact that the driver was wearing camouflage. Hunter or mercenary? Only a search and interrogation could tell.

After 12 hours of driving, we decided we would spend our first night in Neepawa, Manitoba. We unwound in a whirlpool, ate Subway for dinner, and ended our night with a Moosehead beer at Monster Ball saloon. A perfect single moment.

## Giving Your Clients Permission to Live

I heard Roy Diliberto, former Financial Planning Association (FPA) president and author of *Financial Planning—the Next Step: A Practical Approach to Merging Your Clients' Money with Their Lives,* tell a story that helped me to realize the role a financial advisor can play in helping clients to capture beautiful, meaningful moments in life. He shared a story of a long time client who, upon Roy's urging to talk about "something he always wanted to do" shared with Roy his dream of taking his entire family on an elaborate European vacation. He described in vivid detail where they would go and what they would do.

When the client finished describing his cherished dream Roy asked, "Well, why don't you schedule it?"

"Oh," his client responded, "it will cost way too much and will throw my financial plan way out of whack."

Roy asked if he had a good idea of his cost and the client indicated that it would be around $50,000, a considerable sum by most standards. Roy told his client that he would do some homework, run some numbers, and tell him whether or not such a trip would jeopardize his financial future. Roy instinctively picked up on the fact that this client needed his permission to capture one of the most meaningful experiences of his life.

Roy met with him shortly thereafter and told him to start booking his trip because it wouldn't make that much difference and the trade-off would be immeasurable. Roy's advice was poignant because it was an expression of qualitative wisdom based on a quantitative exercise and interpretation.

Roy understood that his client simply needed permission to live.

## The Great Alaskan Highway Ride:
## Day Two—Saskatoon by Afternoon

As we hit mile marker 1,131, we were trying to change lanes when suddenly our rig was thrown into a fishtail (the trailer began to whip). Nate's peace officer training immediately kicked in, and in three brief, instinctive adjustments, he steadied our truck and trailer back into the middle of the channel. I stared at him with admiration at his response to this potential crisis. He was playing it cool on the outside, but I knew he was managing some high blood pressure at the moment.

"Wow, nice work," was all I could say.

"Your training just takes over," he told me with a veteran calm that belied his age.

We gave this road the name of "The Bi-polar Express'" because all day long it would inexplicably turn from sheets of ice to dry runways inviting take-off and the redemption of lost time.

We each drove in three-hour shifts, two shifts each per day. The co-pilot in the passenger seat was responsible for turning the pages of the TripTik from AAA to keep us current and to watch for potential sites of interest.

Dell McCurry sang, about living the simple country life and being a "combread lovin' country boy."

This was Nate. Raised in town but with an internal compass pulling him into the wild, lover of nature and at peace in a duck marsh or a pond. I love the outdoors and nature, but the only hunting and fishing I ever really did was with this son. It was a great way to discover his world.

As the miles passed and bluegrass played and we went through a tacit duel over temperature control in the short cab of his Ford truck, we were experiencing a mild melding of cultures: music, room temperature, a young man fighting youth, and a middle-aged man fighting age.

We decided we would spend our second night in Edmonton, and eat Boston Pizza. We had our eyes focused on making the halfway point by noon tomorrow. More of that single moment.

## A Day that Never Came

My friend Mark told me a story of his aunt and uncle, who had never taken a vacation, worked two jobs for years, saved all they could, and talked of the day when they would turn 62, retire, buy an RV, and "really start living." "My aunt had a stroke two weeks into the retirement and the RV never left the driveway," Mark told me, "and that's one mistake I won't be making. I'm going to do a good bit of living while I'm young enough to enjoy it."

An old acquaintance, Cal, told me about his neighbor, a dairy farmer. He was 45 years old, had just found out he had cancer of the liver, and now was faced with his own mortality. In all his adult years, this dairy farmer had never taken a single day off. An adage among livestock farmers is that "cows don't take days off" and many, not willing to entrust the chores to a hired hand, chain themselves to the operation 24/7, 365 days a year. This farmer had never left for a weekend in Minneapolis, never taken his children and wife on a vacation, never taken a single day to treat his kids to the thrills of an amusement park. There simply was no time for such distractions in his distorted view of how life worked. Now he regretted it, and it was too late.

This farmer's tragic and personal epiphany is similar to the social awareness we all experienced as a result of 9/11. Suddenly, each of us realized how short life could be, and many of us began to see things in a different way.

## The Great Alaskan Highway Ride: Days Three and Four—Taking a Dip in Minus 20

The next two days, driving through the northern Rockies and the Northwest Territories, would prove to be the most tense and intensely spectacular time on our voyage. On the third day, with more than 14 hours of driving behind us, we saw a cement patch one time! The rest of the time we traversed winding and pitched mountain highway on snow and ice with speeds ranging from 25 to 55 mph.

We kept pushing because we had great hopes of taking a swim in –25°F, an experience we had circled on the map as soon as we charted the trip. We had noticed on our map a natural mineral spring and were determined to experience it. After eight hours of white-knuckle navigation, the timing could not have been better. We parked and hiked about one-half mile to the spring where we (very quickly) got undressed and jumped into the 120°F waters. What a moment! Soon, with the combination of heat and vapors and the frigid air around us, we were wearing ice bonnets on our head. After a half hour, the springs had done their work upon our weary bodies and we jumped out and tried drying before we iced over and ran back to the truck for another six hours of snow mountain steering. The next day would make up for the tension of the mountain drive as we came upon scenes that seemed too beautiful to be real.

There were the translucent azure streams with a hue and appearance straight out of Narnia. We had never seen anything like it. The streams ran beside the highway for hours, as did the caribou and other northern mammals. I can't recall where we spent the third night—only that it was literally in the middle of nowhere.

## Making Moments in Life

What are the top two or three things you hope to do while you can?

Is there one experience you've always dreamed of arranging?

These questions could act as conversational levers for bringing clients closer to making their dream a reality. Once your client has answered the first question, your next question might be, "What's holding you back from arranging this now?"

If the answer is "money," it's your turn to step in and demonstrate both the possibilities and the potential trade-offs.

Here are some ideas I've heard as a result of this type of conversation:

- I've always wanted to take a baseball park tour with my dad and son together—three generations that love the game.
- I want to take my parents to Scotland to tour old castles.
- I want take my mother to her parents' homeland.
- I want to take my dad to an old-timers fantasy camp.
- My wife and I want to visit Hong Kong.
- I want to spend two weeks in Maui.
- We want to go on a cruise, first class.
- I want to go on a golfing trip to Ireland.
- I want to take a two-month tour of the Orient.
- I want to tour Europe by train.
- I want to spend a summer in Paris.

And so it goes: whims, wishes, and ideas. But they all hold a special place and will become more special with planning and will become sacred with the doing. These ideas usually require a significant investment of time and money, but they are well worth the effort.

As someone who helped make this single moment a reality, you will hold a special place in your clients' hearts for having given them permission to follow their dreams.

## The Great Alaskan Highway Ride: Waving to Santa in North Pole, Alaska

The final day of our trip would begin at −40°F (which we learned was also −40°C, the single point on which they agree). We drove in the early morning hours along the edge of a 65-mile-long lake and were thrilled to find a gas station along our route with both gasoline and hot coffee. The proprietor took one look at our truck and knew for certain we were novices and prepared a cardboard shield for our radiator, saying, "You won't make it much farther in these temperatures without this. Don't think you'll want to be stranded on this highway at this time of year." Don't suppose we do. We wrote "Fairbanks or bust" on the cardboard and were on our way.

The man at the station had informed us that, although it was more barren and treacherous to drive at this time of year, it was a much smoother ride. He told us that driving this highway in the summer was like bouncing up and down on waves because of the heaving due to extreme congealing and expansion of the road between seasons. The snow and ice filled the road in and made it smooth sailing. We were happy for our good fortune. Could we tolerate 12-hour-long amusement park nausea? We could not.

Within 350 miles, Fairbanks was appearing on the road signs. The last town we would pass through before our arrival was North Pole, a place where the bulk of Santa's mail gets sent. We were too tired to stop and visit, so we simply waved on our way through, jotting down St. Nick's ZIP code as we passed.

Seeing Fairbanks immediately shocked us back into civilization. It is an old oil town, rough and tumble in appearance, and quite a shift for the eyes and soul after staring at ice-bound tundra majesty for hundreds of miles before arriving. We found Nate's 450-square-foot cabin cloaked by five acres of woods, with no running water. I knew immediately that here, in this remote wilderness, he would be in his glory.

My back was killing me from almost 60 hours in the cramped truck cab. The cost was under $3,000, including Nate's moving expenses and my plane ticket home. I had heard enough bluegrass to last me a lifetime.

And I was so grateful I had taken the time to make this trip.

Some people need to spend money to experience such a moment in their life, others need time, and most need both. All require a purposeful allocation, and permission from you to make it happen. Help your clients make the investment. They will never forget what you did for them.

## ReSOULution

Give clients the "permission" they seek to live out those moments they have hoped for, even if it means moving money out for the time being.

# CHAPTER 18

# The Parental Pension

*Honor your mother and father that it may be well with and that you may live long on the earth.*
—The Second Commandment, Exodus

My brother and I were nervous as we sat down for lunch with Dad on his 65th birthday. We had rehearsed this moment in conversation but didn't know how to start it. We knew we were about to enter a strange phase of life involving some role reversals that would put both children and parent in unchartered waters. We had decided to give our father a *parental pension.*

Our father is a hardworking man who spent a career in broadcast journalism. He was a loyal company man whose company did not return the fidelity. In the course of being with one station for over 25 years, he experienced ownership changes five times. The net/net to Dad was that he was now receiving a pension check of $52 every three months for all his services.

He had his Social Security. He was working two part-time jobs (not grudgingly—he knows he would be miserable if he were just sitting around watching his navel grow). He had a very decent lifestyle, even without receiving the proper pension. What Dad didn't have was a margin of comfort, or of safety for that matter. A modest pension would have given him that.

My brother and I had discussed Dad's situation many times. Our emotions ranged from outrage over what had happened to guilt over the lifestyle we were able to enjoy, and ended in a place of gratitude for all our parents had done for us. It was then that we realized that we were in a position to provide the margin of comfort so critical to someone's quality of life in the autumn years.

My brother and I carried no illusions or pretenses about the level of material blessing that had come to our lives. We could trace a lot of our material blessings to living in an unusual era of material opportunity (the 1990s). A grateful sense of obligation began to creep into our conversations about our parents. We knew it was time to honor them. In Dad's case, it was an opportunity not only to honor but to right a wrong as well. We sensed that all the moral lessons they had taught us as children were now coming full circle.

We decided to pool some assets and place them in an investment vehicle that would send a monthly distribution of a few hundred dollars to Dad that would continue for the rest of his life. We had also decided to do the same for our mother when she turned 65 as well. Now, here at lunch on his 65th birthday, we had to find a way to tell him what we had done.

I began by talking about his pension and how it disturbed us that something like that was allowed to happen in corporate transfers. My brother then began to turn the corner by saying, "Dad, we have decided to do something. We want you to listen to us, and we're telling you now that we won't take 'no' for an answer." Dad's eyes looked puzzled and a bit disoriented. My brother went on to describe the arrangement.

Nothing could have prepared us for that moment. How do you prepare yourself for the sight of your father weeping into his lunch? "I don't know what to say," he choked out, "no one has ever taken care of me."

And, indeed, no one truly ever had. He was abandoned by his father at age two. His natural mother shipped him off to five different foster homes by the age of seven. When she finally attempted to raise him herself, she was ill-prepared, often drunk and harsh. He fended for himself from age seven on, selling newspapers and doing errands. As an adult, he had sacrificed for his own family, raised five kids on a lean salary, and learned to be content with little. Now, suddenly, he was on the receiving end and didn't quite know how to take it. But we insisted he take it.

I'll never forget the look in his eyes that day. "I'm a rich man," they said. We all embraced and went on with our lives—my brother and I with a greater appreciation of what it means to be a son, and our father with a greater degree of comfort in his day-to-day living.

Two years later we did the same for mother. We experienced the same joyful weeping, the same sense of reversal, and the same passage. Her situation also involved investing some money so she could build a retirement home near her lifelong friends. (Studies show that possessing a strong social network is a predominant key to successful aging.) Now both parents are receiving their parental pensions.

It took the help of a financial advisor to make this passage a reality. It was my financial planner who helped sort through the various options for directing income into our parents' lives, wading through tax consequences and stability issues and insuring that the money would never run out. In fact, because he is the administrator for our parnental pensions, the checks originate each month from our planner's office—a check that we know brings joy each time it arrives.

## Pocket Money

On a recent phone call to a leader in Asian financial services I was informed that the issue of doing something to help out parents is one of the first that surfaces with financial advisors. They call it "creating pocket money" so their parents don't have to feel so constricted during their retirement lifestyle, so they can feel the liberty to go out and enjoy a meal or a movie with regretting it.

Whether we call it the parental pension dialogue or the pocket money dialogue, it remains a conversation that isn't happening enough in North American financial services practices. For so long the financial services industry has developed only dialogues that are tethered to a maypole product. If there were not a specific product to sell, there was no need for a conversation. Consequently, the "helping parents" conversation rarely treads beyond a long-term care insurance discussion, which is really as much in the interest of the children (and eventual estate) as it is in the interest of their parent(s).

Next-generation advisors draw their dialogues not from a product tank but from a strategic well of life. The wise advisor knows, understands, and empathizes with the emotional issues that weigh upon clients as they course through their various life stages. What middle-aged person has not thought about their parents' well-being and comfort as they watch them retire and begin to age?

Unlike the Asian community, this parental concern is not at the forefront of financial conversations in the United States. You would think that the fact that we are not pursuing this conversation ought to, as a culture, make us blush. Or should it? According to a survey conducted by the AARP, baby boomers are not talking much about the "sandwich generation" issues, but instead are quietly attending to them. Is it possible that the "me" generation is becoming the "us" generation? A glance at the statistics would say yes:

- About 50 percent of boomers ages 45 to 55 have both parents and children at home.
- Twenty-five percent are caring in some way for their elders.
- Eighty percent are "doing something" to help but don't identify themselves as "caregivers."
- Twenty-five percent think they may one day need to leave their job to attend to a parent.

In a study conducted by the Pew Research Center, and reported in the *Washington Post,* as aging boomers step closer to old age, they are reaching deeper into their pockets to care for elderly parents *and* offspring in their 20s who are struggling to launch their own lives.

These boomers, who constitute a quarter of the nation's population, remain in the "sandwich" years, and a larger percentage than in the past is helping both their parents and adult children financially. The reality is clearly sinking in for the boomer generation: that their retirement dreams will need to a sense of responsibility toward other generations. More and more of these boomers will settle on the idea of doing what they can, while they can, for their aging parents. Time is clearly limited, as is the opportunity to say "thanks."

## Starting the Dialogue

The time has come to become more purposeful about a parental pension. The dialogue can start with a preface as simple as:

> When talking about financial planning, a lot of my clients want to talk about their parents' needs even before their own children's.

How is your parent's situation? Are there any steps you would like to consider taking in their behalf?

Through careful accounting and diligent discovery you may find that:

- Your clients' parents are in better shape than they are and this is not a concern to them.
- Your clients are not sure of their own stability and this has held them back from doing anything to help out a parent.
- Such a thought has never entered their mind, but they like the idea.
- Such a thought has never entered their mind, but they dislike the idea.
- Your clients like the idea but would like suggestions on exactly how to go about helping.
- Your clients would like to help their parents but feel obligated to pay for their children's education and, as a result, can't help.

Every situation is unique and every conversation will be idiosyncratic, but over time you will find yourself advising on an issue that is becoming more prominent in this generation than any that preceded it.

Recently, a financial services executive shared with me the fact that he sometimes felt a bit guilty making the kind of money he did and comparing it with how hard and how long his father had to work to make the same amount that he did in a single year. He grew up in a large family and never had much and felt that his father never wanted his children to experience that feeling. Now he's second-guessing that sentiment. "I hate to admit it," he confessed, "but so far I have managed to raise two children, who now feel a sense of entitlement. Funny how I never had much but never felt like the world owed me anything."

He told me that he has set up a "pocket money" fund for his widowed mother over her objections that it was "extravagant." She learned to enjoy the extra money, something her 30 years of raising 10 children on her husband's schoolteacher's salary had never allowed her to do. Your clients may want to do something similar.

## How Badly Do You Want to Learn?

This two-generation dialogue will soon become common for your sandwich-generation clients who are pondering the prospects of contributing to generations on both sides. Some clients, in the dilemma of having to choose, might consider the advice of an advisor I know, "You might just ask yourself which party has better earning prospects for the future."

The last time I checked there were more student loans available than there were senior living loans.

In my home we have a program where each child knows that they will be responsible for one half of their own college expenses. We call it the "Anthony Family Matching Grant College Savings Plan." We are not concerned with how the children fund their side of the deal. They can work in the summer, save ahead, work toward scholarships or grants, or even take out a student loan. The premium on our plan is on industriousness, focus, and ingenuity.

We want them to have some skin in the game as opposed to going through school on the "Budweiser scholarship," which we observed so many of their peers partaking in. Casual observation backs up what statistics demonstrate regarding 19-year-olds and their struggles to focus and perform in college environments: having Dad pay all the bills only exacerbates the potential party problems.

Some parents look at us appalled when we explain our plan, with a tone and look that says, "You're robbing your children of opportunity!" but we disagree: our experience so far has been encouraging.

My two oldest children took a year off right after high school to work "in the real world" and earned some money while they decided the direction they wanted to take in education (a move that would cause panic for many parents and school counselors). The welcome and unintended consequence of this decision was that they both came to the quick realization of how their prospects in the world looked without a college education and didn't like what they saw. As a parent, I could not have hand-picked a greater motivational lesson for either of them.

Our first son soon went to work on earning an education grant while working in a special program with the Department of Natural Resources so he would be able to pursue his education in wildlife management and law enforcement. As mentioned in the last chapter, today he is a natural resources officer in Alaska. When he graduated, his entire education was paid in full.

My second son is in the process of pursuing his education and is personally invested in the process as well. I understand that every parent must choose their own path in helping their children. We have made the decision to allow them the struggle of paying some price to get the education they need and have also chosen to tell them about the financial aid we have chosen to send our parents' way as well because of their participation.

## A Little Goes a Long Way

Financial planner Bruce Bruinsma informed me that studies show that most seniors say they would feel a greater level of comfort with just an additional $300 to $400 per month. Many of these individuals feel the compression of rising health care costs, household and lifestyle maintenance costs, rising utilities, and static income. In this equation a little bit goes a long way—a long way toward going on a short trip, a long way toward a special night out once in a while, a long way toward some entertainment and fun, a long way toward peace of mind and quality of life.

There are a number of innovative approaches for addressing your clients' parents' quality of life. Briggs Matsko, CFP, told me that developers in retirement areas are beginning to build homes with casitas ("little houses") included behind the main houses on the same property. These casitas have smaller floor plans, with an independent kitchen, living room, bathroom, and bedrooms for people who want to help their parents but respect their need to "not become a burden" and to have their own privacy. Both parties can come and go as they wish without feeling they are suffocating or being suffocated.

Here are some other ways children have helped provide a parental pension. You may wish to adapt these into your own practice:

- Purchasing long-term care policies for their parents, protecting both their parent's estate and their own.
- Hiring a retired parent to work as many hours as they wish in their business, meeting both an economic and an emotional dilemma (the need to feel useful and engaged).
- Paying a parent's assisted-living expenses so they can remain in their own home.

Demographics and longer life expectancies portend a world where parents and their grown children's lives will be physically, geographically, and materially intertwined. If this possibility is not at the forefront of your client's conversation, it almost certainly is in the back of their mind.

Not every client will want, need, or be in a position to make a financial move in favor of a parent. But introducing this dialogue is a smart thing to do for your business when one looks at the demographics ahead. It is also an honorable thing to do.

You have an opportunity to help many in this generation meet real needs and to say "thanks." The gift that many baby boomers give will one day circle back to them through their children. After all, what greater gift could we give to our children (and to ourselves) than the example of how to honor one's parents?

There are few moments in my life that can compare to the parental pension conversation on Dad's 65th birthday. I don't ever remember a moment where so much was said with so little spoken. It was communicated from the soul through the eyes. We saw a change in Dad's eyes after the initial stun of gratitude had sunk in, a look like he had just received the greatest payoff of his life, not in material terms, but in knowing that he had raised his children right.

### ReSOULution

Give your clients the opportunity to express their concern for their parents' futures—bring strategic creativity to the conversation. By making the decision to not allow this stone to go unturned, you can help your clients do something meaningful with their means and reap a dividend for life.

# 19

# By The Side of the Road

## DEALING WITH THE BIG "WHAT IF . . ."

*There is that person who sells to a client what they do not need; this is an integrity issue. Equal in harm is the person who fails to sell what the client truly needs; this is a matter of accountability.*
—Mitch Anthony

A regional manager for a major financial services company was bemoaning the fact that his advisors were leaving disability insurance sales on the table. It seemed that out of 800 total agents in this territory, his advisors were selling the fewest number of policies. While he grumbled about the money his company wasn't making because of his advisors' inattention to the issue, I began to think about this issue from the other side of the table (the client's side), and began to ponder how much risk the advisors were leaving on the table for their clients.

How many homes did the average advisor serve? A few hundred? For the sake of illustration, let's assume that the average advisor served 500 homes and multiply that by the 800 advisors in this territory, and our illustration now represents 400,000 homes. Out of these 400,000 homes, a few disability policies came through each month, which totaled approximately 200 policies at the end of the year.

## Helping Your Clients Do the Right Thing

By this example are we to assume that less than 1 percent of the population *needs* disability insurance? Of course not. This is a breach of duty by those commissioned to help consumers face reality regarding our risks. Are we so consumed now with not selling to consumers what they do not want that we now fail to sell to them what they truly need? Dangers exist for consumers at both ends of the pendulum. I almost wonder if the latter isn't more debilitating than the former.

Consider the following:

- According to the Disability Insurance Resource Center (DIRC), if you are over 35 years of age, the chances of your becoming disabled before age 65 are 2.2 to 3.3 times greater than dying (depending on your age). In fact, if you are 35 years old, there is a 50 percent chance that you'll become disabled for 90 days or longer before you reach age 65 (and a 33 percent chance if you're 50). Compare that to the odds of totaling your car (1 in 250), or losing your home to catastrophe (1 in 1,200).
- The current subprime mortgage crisis notwithstanding, DIRC estimates that 48 percent of all mortgage foreclosures in this country are caused by disability. Only 3 percent are caused by death.
- DIRC reports that the average disability policy covers 50 percent to 60 percent of a worker's gross income, meaning even those of us who receive disability insurance as a company benefit may be underinsured unless we can survive on 50 percent to 60 percent of our gross income.
- According to the Consumer Federation of America (www.consumerfed.org), 82 percent of American workers either don't have long-term disability coverage or believe what they have is inadequate. That means only 18 percent or less of Americans either have coverage or feel they have enough.

There are a couple of reasons why advisors are not doing a better job of engaging their clients in a discussion about the merits of disability insurance:

1. Advisors are conscientious to the point of no longer pressing upon a client a legitimate solution to a genuine problem.

2. Advisors don't know how to hold a meaningful dialogue around the topic of disability.

I also think advisors are failing to hold clients accountable to act in their own best interests. Yes, you read that right—*accountable.* I believe a good advisor first helps clients become *aware* of the issue and second, holds that client accountable to act in his own best interest. Competent and caring risk managers do not let people slide by with excuses and evasions that are rooted in human nature's worst features: procrastination, feelings of invincibility, and denial. When faced with these impediments to safety, the caring advisor must learn to engage in a more courageous conversation.

## The Persistence of a Caring Professional

Mark had reviewed Sam's insurance coverages and was concerned that Sam, in his early 60s, had neglected to give serious attention to his level of life insurance. At the current level of coverage, his untimely death would cause certain hardship for his family-owned business. Mark emphatically stated this in Sam's review and watched as Sam dismissively waved him off, "Yeah, yeah, I'm fine."

That night, Mark tossed and turned, thinking about Sam. Not that he had a premonition, but he felt Sam needed to understand the serious threat to his estate. He went back to see Sam the next day and rearticulated his concerns.

Sam said, "I'll think about it," which Mark knew from experience meant no.

Three days later, Mark stopped in again. Sam greeted him with, "Now whaddya want?"

Mark said, "I'm not leaving here until you sign this application and get this situation where it needs to be for your wife and family."

Sam finally acceded, saying, "I will if you promise to get off my back."

A few weeks later, while driving down a country road, Mark happened upon a one-car accident that had just taken place. The Lincoln Continental was turned over. Mark thought the Lincoln Continental looked vaguely familiar, so he jumped out of his car to see if he could be of any help. When he looked in the overturned vehicle, he saw Sam, dead of a heart attack.

The very fact that you get paid for providing the service or products you provide will always leave open the door of cynicism in the client's mind. Sam thought Mark was just trying to make a sale, but Mark persisted because he knew his motives transcended Sam's opinion of his motives. Genuine, sincere motives such as those possessed by Mark fuel an inexhaustible supply of persistence.

Mark didn't persist in selling the life insurance to Sam to satisfy his wallet; he persisted in order to placate his heart. He had the foresight to estimate the potential risks for Sam's family business and family well-being, and he had the tenacity to persist against vaporous objections.

This brings me to my next point about the legitimate sale of a product because of a genuine need. Objections arise in legitimate situations because the script advisors are asked to use presses the objection to the surface. These scripts fail to find any emotionally relevant anchor in the life and well-being of the client. Instead, you need to engage your client in what I call the financial life dialogue, a conversation that is footed in life's realities, evokes awareness, and allows the client to decide (with emotional clarity) what sort of decision they need to make.

## An Example

For context: disability insurance may be the most erroneously named product in the risk management market. Like long-term care insurance, shouldn't it describe what it provides? If products are going to be named after the event that triggers them, then life insurance needs to be called death insurance. Because it doesn't describe what it provides. Disability insurance is really income insurance. Disability insurance is to living what life insurance is to dying. They are both designed to protect your family's income and lifestyle in the case of a mishap.

> *Question 1:* What are your most valuable skill set and capabilities? (Get specific; don't take "I'm a doctor" for an answer. It's her brain, her hands, etc., that must come to the surface.)
>
> *Question 2:* How well are you compensated for each of these skills and capabilities?
>
> *Question 3:* Can you think of any scenarios that could keep you from being able to use these skills?
>
> *Questions 4:* If you were somehow disabled, who would suffer the most impact and how?

*Questions 5:* How much protection is enough protection for you and the lifestyle you want to protect?

## Physician, Heal Thyself

Two observations I have made in teaching financial professionals are as follows:

1. Advisors begin selling more disability insurance to those who need it because they experience a sense of "clearing," that is, permission to be assertive when you see a client riding their bicycle toward a cliff. When integrity meets empathy, there is little resistance on the part of the provider or the purchaser.
2. Many advisors themselves are underinsured. A smarter company would have brought applications to the training because almost 50 percent of the advisors present were ready to improve their own risk protection by the time they talked through the above questions!

This phenomenon begs an obvious point and a more subliminal point. The obvious point is that you are not going to have a whole lot of conviction about something you don't "own" in the literal and emotional sense. The more subliminal point is my thought about advisors who do not have advisors. They are like the physicians who treat themselves. These advisors have lost the benefits of objectivity and observation.

One advisor said that he became keenly aware, while talking about question 4, that disability and resulting financial hardship would cost him and his wife a core value in their life, that of raising their own children. In his case, he decided that disability insurance was "core-value insurance." In fact, disability insurance became ability insurance—the ability to raise his own children.

Another told a story about a lawyer I know who was suddenly afflicted with a degenerative mental disease out of the blue; her business interests and entire income disappeared. Art, a 36-year veteran, wondered aloud about what disabled people thought about during the day and how much financial stress was part of that thinking.

These stories reflect the fact that a good dialogue is not about steering or manipulating people; it is about raising awareness.

Once awareness is raised, your client must make the final decision. Steering and manipulating is the work of amateurs.

Food for thought: medical and drug advances are a two-edged sword. The things that used to kill you now only disable you but have the potential to kill you financially.

## Storyselling

If you've already read my book *Storyselling for Financial Advisors* (Kaplan Business, 2000), consider this a refresher. Storyselling is communicating to the right side of the brain. The right side of the brain ignores numbers, comparisons, and linear logic. It does, however, respond to a story. This is the place where the decision trigger is housed in the brain. When the right side of the brain *feels* comfortable or justifiably moved, the client moves from nodding to signing. We often fail to sell products and services that our clients desperately need because we do not appeal to the right side of the brain. Instead of telling a story of numbers, we need to begin telling a number of stories.

There are two aspects to storyselling:

1. Getting your clients story' (this is accomplished through the financial life dialogue we already spoke about).
2. Telling your story with the use of the analogy and metaphor. Metaphors take the language of the known and use it to explain the unknown. When professionals use "features and benefits" to try to convince clients, they often lose the client's interest because the jargon used to describe the features and benefits doesn't mean anything—it's the language of the company or the industry.

Following are some examples of illustrations and analogies useful for explaining disability insurance and its usefulness.

### Metaphors in Action

- *The Financial Airbag.* "Disability or *income* insurance is kind of like the airbag in a car. It can play a role in preventing an accident from becoming a catastrophe. It doesn't erase the fact that the accident happened but can help minimize a bad situation."

- *The Auxiliary Generator.* "Do you know anyone who has an auxiliary generator? Why would we have one of those in our home? For those who live in the colder regions, it is because we don't want to awaken to a temperature of 20 degrees on a cold winter night. It's there to keep our family out of the cold and dark in the case of a power loss. Disability insurance is like an auxiliary generator for your family finances."
- *The Guaranteed Contract.* "Athletes have guaranteed contracts for a couple of reasons: (1) they know they are one quick step away from a career-ending disability; and (2) they understand how closely tied their income is to their skill sets and how great the impact to their lifestyle would be if the flow of that income were impeded. Obviously, your job may not have the inherent risks that an athlete does, but we do need to examine the relationship between your skill sets and income and how much interruption you could justifiably tolerate."

This final analogy and dialogue is what I would characterize as a *courageous conversation*. Courageous is defined as "being able to deal with danger or fear without flinching." It takes sufficient courage suffused by truly caring to confront clients with the fact that the biggest threat to their security may be staring them in the mirror.

## Your Financial House and the Winds of Destruction

"This is your financial house, and what we have learned is that there are four winds that have the potential to destroy this house. From the north is the cold wind of death, which, of course, can devastate the house. We can fence out those winds with life insurance. From the south comes Uncle Sam and his tax policies that over time can wreak havoc on the house. We can fence out those winds with good tax management. From the west come the tornado-like winds of market volatility and the damage they can do in a short time to years' worth of building. We can hedge against those winds with proper diversification. Finally, from the east come the winds of catastrophe, accident, and disability. We build a fence around those winds by insuring your income stream.

One part of my business is helping people build wealth. Another aspect is helping people protect that wealth from these winds of destruction. Experience has taught me, however, that I'm also in

the business of helping people protect themselves from themselves. We are all subject to human nature, and nothing is more common to human nature than to look at something we should do and to think or say things like:

"I'll do it later when it's more convenient." This is **procrastination**. We say it but have no system of accountability to hold ourselves to.

"It won't happen to me." This is the **propensity to gamble**. What makes us think we can stand at the craps table of life and never throw a seven?

"I'll be fine." This is **denial** and **wishful thinking**. As if not thinking about it insures it won't happen and the idea that all our life events will follow a "best-case" scenario.

"I consider it to be my job to make you aware of the risks, have a dialogue about those risks, and, finally, to hold you accountable to your own best intentions. So, if you tell me you want to protect your income, I'm going to follow through and persist until that protection is in place."

*There is in the act of preparing the moment we start caring.*
—Winston Churchill

You can't engage in this sort of dialogue without genuine concern for your client's well-being. They will sense that concern and will be compelled to act in their own best interests. Too many people in this country are left in a vulnerable state because their agent or advisor has not offered such a dialogue or has failed to hold clients accountable to their best intentions.

You can try to sell insurance products, or you can serve clients by having a heart-to-heart dialogue about risk. If you choose the former, you hit targets you should have missed and, worse, miss targets you should have hit. Should you choose the latter, you will be prepared and be able to live with yourself should you ever find your client on the side of the road.

## ReSOULution

Don't allow your clients to take unnecessary and easily resolved risks. Courageously confront their denial, negligence, and hubris with stories of what life can do to the best of intentions and focus on the people who will be most affected should life take an unexpected turn.

# 20

# A 100 Percent Certainty

*O death where is thy sting? O grave where is thy victory?*
—Paul's letter to Corinth

It has been said that there are only two certain things in life: death and taxes.

Actually, there's a third that's a hybrid between the two: taxes after death. And not just those administrated by the government.

It is not just your client's estate that is being taxed—their survivors' lives are as well. While plenty has been written about estate planning, and most of you are probably already discussing this with your clients, not enough is being done. Too many of you are letting your clients put off crucial planning that they simply don't want to deal with. A lack of preparation, foresight, and obviation are the grave's final victory. To answer Paul's rhetorical prose one might say that the great sting of death is in the financial hardship too often left behind.

These days it seems like I'm finding myself going to a lot of funerals and seeing one unexpected death one after another. There is very little one can do to "prepare" for death at the emotional and spiritual levels. When it comes, it will do unexpected things to our being and we'll need to labor our way through. The exception to this rule, however, is the financial ramifications of death. Following are some recent death-related observations and associated fiscal laments:

- A man dies suddenly at age 63 leaving behind an unintended scavenger hunt for financial records, adding confusion and fear of poverty to every other burden the family bears.
- A former schoolteacher in her 70s precedes her unhealthy husband in death. He loses the $1,800 dollars per month from her state pension because she assumed he would precede her and chose only the life insurance option in the pension plan.
- A young man with three young children dies and leaves enough life insurance to pay for his funeral and a trip to Disney World.
- A middle-aged family man dies in an accident and has no life insurance, no will, and scattered records.

I'm assuming you have seen these types of stories yourself and some scenarios that are much worse. One such story came awfully close to home with the passing of Gene, one of the team members in our business. Had it not been for the unrelenting reminders and loving harassment of Lori, a former member of our team, Gene's progeny would have been left in a severe financial situation.

About a year and a half ago Gene applied for life insurance and was denied because of his weight. Lori made it her weekly mission to remind Gene of the promise he had made to himself (and to his two small children) to lose the weight and insure his family against his own mortality. Some people might not have possessed the urgency that motivated Lori, seeing that Gene was youthful, a nonsmoker, and quite athletic. But Lori spent many years in the life insurance industry and knows that life offers no guarantees equal to death.

Lori called me one afternoon sobbing with the horrible news that Gene had passed away in his sleep of an aneurysm. He was 37 years old. He simply went to bed and never woke up. Lori was saying something else, but I couldn't understand it through her tears.

"Say that again, Lori," I asked.

"He was approved just two months ago. He had finally lost the 20-plus pounds and he had life insurance for his kids. I nagged him every week for over a year, and he finally did it."

A close call that would have become a tragic financial epitaph for a man with a CFP if not for one simple factor: another human being possessing enough compassion, foresight, and fortitude to assist Gene to do what he truly wanted to do.

## Exit Ramp 279

Very few people are properly prepared for one of the 100 percent certainties of life and of this business, that you will die, and there is a significant chance that that there will be no road signs telling you the time and place. This is not like a trip to Wall Drug in South Dakota, where the signs start appearing 500 miles out and reminders pop up every 25 miles or so. No, death has a mind of its own and extends no forgiveness for those in denial and those who procrastinate toward preparation.

I'm coming to the point where I believe that the pin needed to pop the balloon of denial is a simple phrase loaded on the lips of good advisors.

Everyone, *"this is not about you! It's about the people you'll leave behind and the position you will leave them in."* And this message needs to be repeated until action is taken and each client fulfills their best intentions.

I recently listened to Dr. Moshe Milevsky from the Individual Finance and Insurance Decisions Centre quote these salient facts from a National Bureau of Economic Research study based on data from the Health and Retirement Study.

- "People's perceptions of their own mortality risks are systematically biased. . . ."
- ". . . Many people respond with a 0 percent or 100 percent when asked to estimate the odds for living 20 more years. . . ."
- ". . . People with relatively low life expectancies tend to be overly **optimistic,** and people with relatively high life expectancy tend to be overly **pessimistic.** . . ."

## Mortality Combat

What these facts illustrate is that people are nowhere near the center of gravity when it comes to their own mortality. How can one say that there is a 100 percent chance that they will be around in 20 more years? The people who need to worry most are living life with rose-colored glasses. What this means for you is that more intent and resilience is required toward confrontation with the inevitable.

I have a deep suspicion that the context for this conversation needs to change in order to gain traction leading to action. Until we make it simpler to initiate this discussion and more user friendly to accomplish the needed objectives, clients will "stay away in droves," to quote an old Yogi Berra-ism. The most popular context currently offered for this life/death conversation is *estate planning*, but this discussion has compound limitations:

- Many people think that they do not have an "estate"; that's something only the very wealthy are concerned with.
- The term *estate planning* is a sterile, legal term that evokes images of complexity rather than emotions of urgency.
- Because of tax and legal implications, accountants and attorneys are pulled into the discussion leading to intimidation for some clients and fear of expense for others.

## Your Own FEMA Crisis

An alternative I would like to offer you to help you solve your clients' lack of preparedness and accompanying denial, to be used as a preface to an estate planning conversation, is an emergency management discussion. Nobody is foolish enough to think they are exempt from the unpredictable crisis visiting their life and family. We'll call this client discussion the family emergency management dialogue.

Your introduction of this concept to your clients can come in the form of a fairly recent event that they are all familiar with: Hurricane Katrina.

When Hurricane Katrina devastated New Orleans and the Gulf Coast, everyone was shocked by the impact, but no one was truly surprised that such an event could take place. In fact, it was an oft-discussed and journaled fact of inevitability with those who made their home there. It wasn't as much a matter of "if" but "when," especially with those in the know. We, as onlookers, were as appalled at the lack of an organized and orchestrated response to this crisis as we were by the material and emotional desolation. Then, as reports surfaced regarding repeated warnings about the breached levees, we were left wondering, "Why didn't they do something ahead of this crisis?"

Strange, isn't it, how your clients can separate themselves from similar impending realities in their own personal lives?

Consider the foreknowledge that had been brought to the attention of local, state, and federal administrations that the levee's design, developed by the Army Corp of Engineers, was flawed. That video shot by the local fire department shows the levee being broken by water pressure (that could have come from any rainstorm—it just happened to coincide with Katrina) before it spilled over. Reports have surfaced that officials were warned on several occasions of the flaws in the levee, yet nothing was done. A crack appeared, the ground was soon soaked, and Katrina appeared and was given the weight of blame that could have been avoided proactively.

There was plenty of time and manifold opportunity to obviate the obvious and realistic fate of a city in a crater on a hurricane coast. It was going to happen, and it is somewhat amazing that it didn't visit sooner. Life will never be the same for those who lived there and will never live there again. Life is much different now.

America found a convenient scapegoat for its frustration with the lack of preparedness of the administrator of the Federal Emergency Management Agency (FEMA), Michael Brown. Most of us will long remember the reports of his being more concerned about his appearance and wardrobe than he was for the situation at hand.

He was, by most accounts, inept and the wrong person for the job, but was by no means alone in this description. There was an entire line-up of individuals at all levels of local, state, and federal government who could justifiably shoulder culpability for their lacking sense of urgency and foresight, not to mention their inability to mobilize response.

At this point in this conversation I would like to begin to draw personal parallels with the preparedness and concerns of the average client in their family emergency response plan:

- People know that there is a 100 percent risk of the "levee of life" being breached and that they will be carried away.
- They may be more concerned with stuff, appearances, and everyday activity than they are with this inevitable risk.
- People understand that when they die it is not they who are left to hardship and suffering.

## A Different Sort of Dialogue

Let's imagine sitting down with clients with a novel twist on the first phase of estate planning that we are going to call the Family Emergency Management Plan. We begin the conversation with the Katrina/FEMA analogy and say:

> I don't know about you but I was horrified by the damage I saw. People who saw it in person said the ruin was beyond imagination. It was also very disturbing to me to sit and hear that it all could have and should have been prevented. Not just the loss of life through evacuation but the breaching of the levees themselves.
>
> To hear that the city and state and federal officials had been warned repeatedly through the years by scientists and authorities on the matter but continued to put off action is a real tragedy that, having been dealt with in a timely fashion, would have prevented the tragedy we witnessed.
>
> The reason I bring this topic up is that, sadly, I see this scenario of delayed prevention play constantly in my business, but in this particular case it has to do with the possibility of something unfortunate happening to the chief wage earner in a home and how such an emergency would play itself out.

Begin with this metaphorical premise and see how your client responds to it. You know where to take the conversation when they ask what it is they need to do to prepare their Family Emergency Management Plan. Following is the beginning of the FEMP checklist:

1. A life insurance benefit sufficient to maintain the current lifestyle, preserve educational opportunity for children and match inflation during the life expectancy of the chief beneficiary.
2. Centralized point for documentation of all financial records (an area of service that more advisory offices need to begin offering).
3. Contingency plans in case of the deaths of both partners.
4. Planning for long-term disability rather than death.
5. An ethical will, memoir, or the like to leave your story, thoughts, and hopes for those left behind.

If you told your client that you could prove with 100 percent certainty that their company was going to go bankrupt, would they want to sit down with you and prepare? If you told them that you had foolproof evidence that they were about to win the lottery, would they want to plan ahead? Of course, they would. Because of the inevitability of the events, they would be a fool not to.

I'm pretty certain actuarial science will back up the assertion that there is a 100 percent chance that every one of your clients will die (as will you) and there are also pretty darn good odds that the event will catch them by surprise.

Because of the general public's reticence to deal with this certainty, I would maintain that nothing less than evangelistic ardor is required, a Dr. Phil–like propensity for the reality check, the courageous/compassionate confronter, to act as an indefatigable fatalist where death is concerned.

An advisor once told me that he always felt like his job was kind of like the best man at a wedding. He was a witness to the promises being made and would be there down the road to remind the groom of those promises should the need ever arise. This is a perfect metaphor for the deeper responsibilities inherent in the financial profession. Nowhere does this analogy resonate as it does in the realm of mortality.

## Best Intentions

After reading an article I published on this same theme, I received a phone call from my good friend Bobby, a veteran in the financial services industry. He said, "Mitch, I want you to know that at least one of your readers heard what you had to say and did something about it. I realized after hearing about your departed friends that I had no guarantees and have been putting this off needlessly and exposing my family to risk. I made the phone calls I needed to make the set the wheels in motion to get this remedied."

Bobby has a wife and three children under the age of four.

No one intends to leave chaos behind. No one plans to impoverish their mates and children, and no one has a crystal ball. But clients continue to behave as if they do. The dead don't live with the consequences of having dragged their heels. The sting is felt by those left behind.

Will you stand up and hold your clients accountable to those intentions? Will you help them keep their promises? Will you persist as Lori did with Gene until action is taken?

## ReSOULution

Realize that what is needed is a victory of intent, which, sad to say, does not seem to take place for most good people without some level of accountability. Such is the regrettable DNA of the human species. An even greater attribute of the soul is the determination to persist in the pursuit of what we know must be done. For the sake of mercy, hold each client accountable to their best intentions.

# 21

# The New Venture Philanthropy Dialogue

*We must perform a kind of Copernican revolution and give the question of the meaning of life an entirely new twist, to wit: It is life itself that asks questions of man. He should recognize that he is questioned, questioned by life; he has to respond by being responsible; and he can answer to life only by answering for his life.*
—Viktor Frankl, *The Doctor and the Soul*

Alan knew that the gentleman sitting before him was hungry for a conversation beyond the numbers, benchmarks, and planning strategies. He had responded to Alan's advertising of "financial life planning" and the promise of a more meaningful dialogue around money. He spent a good 45 minutes talking about gaining financial satisfaction, achieving life balance, and developing a personal definition of true wealth.

The prospective client, after engaging in these discussions, commented, "This was the best discussion around money I have ever had. But," he added, "you need to know something about me regarding money. I'm not interested in making any more, although I would like to protect what I have from unnecessary taxes. What I would really like you to do," he challenged Alan, *"is help me bring meaning to my money."*

In the course of their dialogue this man mentioned several businesses he owned, which fueled Alan's curiosity. And so he asked the man, "How much money do you have?"

"$1.5 billion," was his answer.

## Bringing Meaning to Your Client's Money

As successful baby boomers ramp up the liquidation of businesses or transition to "doing something more meaningful with their lives," we are going to see an escalating interest in what we would characterize as the *venture philanthropy* dialogue—a conversation about capitalizing (in a philanthropic sense) on your clients' assets, both tangible and intangible. Your business will move from amassing means to building meaning around the means.

This sentiment is growing, and there are not enough advisors in the current marketplace who can meet the demand. Clients are ready to transcend material collections, showpieces, and gain—simply for the sake of gain. These individuals want to elevate their "game" to an altruistic level where they see the investment of their lives and wealth pay transcendent dividends.

The old estate planning dialogue is a dry conversation that doesn't draw them to the table; it's not about leaving a pile to the kids—it's about making a difference in the world—the things they care about, the things they know about—staying connected to your client and their money for the long run.

## Philanthropy Trends

The *Economist* predicted that another golden age of philanthropy is staged to begin in the United States and around the world: "There are signs that a new kind of donor is emerging, with a new approach to giving. That new approach includes being more personally involved with their giving and placing a much higher premium on accountability." As we've seen, in 2006 Bill Gates and Warren Buffett took this approach to a new level.

According to Bruce Meyerson of the Associated Press in an article that appeared in the *Arizona Daily Star,* "While they may not have 26 billion to sock away into a foundation like Bill Gates, many of his fellow boomers won't settle for just writing checks to their favorite charities."

With a first wave of boomers nearing retirement, and many starting to receive inheritance from their parents, a growing number are establishing family foundations with endowments as small as $50,000 to $100,000. According to www.Guidestar.org, nonprofits number 1.5 million and, according to what we're seeing, appear to be growing.

Boomers are opening accounts with community-based foundations and setting up "virtual" foundations with donor-advised funds that allow the individual to decide when, where, and how much to contribute. This idea fits the baby boom generation's approach to life, family, and personal fulfillment (they are figuring out that "giving while you're living" is a part of the fulfillment puzzle). This generation is more hands-on with their giving than their parents were, opting for personal involvement, local charities, and often designing their own approaches for social involvement.

Another sign is the growing popularity of community foundations with total assets of over $3 billion, and the growing popularity of donor fund offerings by firms like Vanguard and Fidelity.

Research on the increase in family foundations by The Foundation Center (reported in *Barron's*) reveals that the number of family foundations grew by over 60 percent between 1998 and 2002 to over 30,000 such foundations. It is worth noting that two-thirds of these family foundations had less than $1 million in assets when the foundations began. It is estimated that the number of American foundations may have doubled from 1990 to 2005.

According to FinancialCounsel.com there is a vast majority of middle-income individuals who make annual gifts based on generosity rather than tax motives. *Case in point:* nonprofits feared an ebb in donations with the advent of the Economic Growth and Tax Relief Reconciliation Act (EGTRRA), which reduced top income tax rates. However, donations actually increased after that tax cut by over $1 billion, which demonstrates that this giving ethos is deeply rooted in the boomer generation.

## Becoming an Eye Witness to Your Own Goodness

A watershed moment in the world of philanthropy came from Charles Feeney, co-founder of Duty Free Shoppers Group, Ltd., who sold his share of the business for $3.5 billion and proceeded to give away all but about $5 million of his personal fortune.

His foundation, Atlantic Philanthropies, announced that it was going to quadruple its distribution of grants from $100 million to $400 million per year in order exhaust the entire endowment in 12 to 15 years! Why such charitable aggression? Feeney capsulized his approach with the now popular phrase he has been credited with coining: he is a believer in *"giving while living."*

Philanthropy once inferred that the donor was dead; but now, it has been expanded to include living donors—and highly involved donors as well, with a bent for highly personalized giving. Individualized expression is the description that captures the boomer ethos. Should it surprise anyone that this group, having created their own individualized career tracks and having borne the responsibility of their own retirement that an unprecedented age of highly personalized giving would be in the waiting?

If you carefully examine the goals and ambitions of highly successful individuals as they phase out of corporate careers, you will find in the vast majority a desire to teach, mentor, help, develop, and create ways of touching lives with the skill sets they have gained in building successful businesses. They are ready to move from success to significance:

- Bill, a retired senior manager from a *Forbes* top 100 company, spent the last three years gaining his CFP so he could provide financial planning for single mothers who couldn't afford it.
- JoEllen, a successful publicist, is trimming her for-profit schedule to part-time in order to help selected charities with her skills and services.
- Joseph, an entrepreneur, is developing football camps throughout the summer as a medium for teaching important life values and is utilizing well-known college coaches and players as drawing cards to attract youth.
- John and Lucy, retired owners of an industry-leading company and heirs to a fortune in the mid-eight figures, spent their time searching out meaningful but struggling charities that were operating "under the radar" of public notoriety. They partnered with these charities financially and as members of their boards to solidify their causes.

Many venture philanthropists are joining forces with others who share their thirst for charity and accountability and are creating novel approaches to age-old problems in local and global settings. Many of these organizations take the "venture capital" business aspects of their approach very seriously by implementing quarterly controls and metrics and holding causes accountable for results.

## CFOs for the New VPs

These stories are endless and yet have just begun to be told. We are entering an age of "signature charity," where benefactors are seeking to leave a unique and indelible fingerprint in causes that have moved their heart. Instead of sending big checks to big charities, the entrepreneurial spirit is driving these individuals to do something different. Which financial professionals or firms will come alongside this wave of compassionate capitalism?

For those who want to ride a meaningful and prosperous wave into the future, I would suggest the examination of the venture philanthropy trend. It is interesting to note that when I wrote the first edition of *The New Retirementality* and suggested the term *venture philanthropy*, I could find no Internet references to the term. Five years later, there are scores of people and groups rallying around the idea. This is not to imply that the book had anything to do with popularizing the term, but instead that the marriage of the words *venture* and *philanthropy* feels instinctive and rings intuitively for this generation.

I am using the term *venture philanthropy* in a much broader sense than the venture capitalist crowd. I'm including the free agent, entrepreneur, and business owner, all of whom are contemplating cashing out or spreading their entrepreneurial instincts toward charity. What is venture philanthropy? It is the utilization of all resources, tangible and intangible, that your clients can bring to bear in the process of actualizing their own philanthropic instincts.

This is a market that will see tremendous growth and reward the tuned-in and purpose-driven advisor with manifold opportunities.

The idea behind the venture philanthropy dialogue is to help clients flesh out:

- The roots of their philanthropic sentiments.
- The causes that most interest them.
- The specialized insights, skills, and visions they have to offer.
- The ultimate good their money can do.

Below are some questions you may ask yourself in order to determine the purpose of your *venture philanthropy*.

**Question 1: "What people or causes have made an impact in your life and in the lives of those you love?"** What we are really asking here is, "Who has helped you along the way?" Or maybe even, "Who do you wish had been there along the way?"

Whether someone was there or not, those associations are indelibly printed in our memory banks and are often at the root of the philanthropic instinct. "Someone was there for me when I really needed help. I want to be there for others." Or, "My father always wanted to be an engineer, but he was too poor and worked common labor his whole life. He always wished his life had turned out differently. I want to help people in that sort of situation."

This is a conversation that is pregnant with possibilities for setting up scholarship funds and specialty foundations. Explore the possibilities and encourage the idea of doing something unique.

**Question 2: "Do you have any ideas for a cause or charity that you think could fill an important need in our world?"** Perhaps you have clients like George and Darryl Thompson, a father and son who share philanthropic pulses. Upon being offered early retirement as a senior-level manager at IBM, George decided to follow his heart with his money, energy, and time. He had always been bothered by racial intolerance in his community and decided to do something about it. He founded The Diversity Council and designed programs for schoolchildren and the workplace promoting tolerance and understanding. The program reaches tens of thousands yearly.

George's son Darryl was looking for something significant to do with his talents and energy after retiring from the NFL. He found his life's work with the Bolder Options program, which mentors inner-city youth who have lacked a positive male role model in their life and have begun to show signs of taking the wrong path. Bolder Options use sporting activities as a forum for building significant relationships and helping change the lives of these youth.

How do you know that the clients sitting before you do not harbor these sorts of philanthropic dreams? You won't know until you ask. Chances are they will also lead you to others just like them.

**Question 3: "What do you have to offer other than your money to help further the causes you believe in?"**    Some years back my step-mother, Muriel, was undergoing treatment for small cell lymphoma and traveling cross-country to the Mayo Clinic four to six times per year for treatment. I saw firsthand how taxing the experience was on both her and my father—financially, physically, and psychologically. The cost of chemotherapy is massive, and it is expensive to fly across the country. I observed the stress the financial issues were bringing to the situation and understood the detrimental effect such stress could produce on the immune system.

Being a frequent flyer, I saw an easy and painless solution: I could give Muriel my World Perks account information and let her be own travel agent with the miles. Muriel and my Dad constantly remarked about the reduced stress and joy of not having to worry about coming up with the funds to get treatment. It was that easy; simply transferring a resource that could serve one party better than another. The last thing I wanted to do after accumulating all those miles was to go on another trip—and so the miles simply stacked up.

A couple of years ago, I happened to mention the idea of actually developing a program like this with the Mayo Clinic. They agreed that it would be beneficial to many of their patients and, as a result *The Rxtra Mile* program was born. This program encourages frequent fliers to donate their miles to help cancer patients get to and from the Mayo Clinic (or another clinic, if they prefer).

There is no telling the breadth and reach of the charitable ideas that can and will be born just by asking this question. Many people have made observations about underserved needs and unjust and inequitable circumstances but could use just a little nudge of encouragement to actually do something about it. That nudge could come from you during this conversation.

**Question 4: "What do you feel is the greatest good that can come from your wealth?"**    Brooks Moneypenny, a successful financial advisor with Morgan-Keegan, believes that the greatest good that can come from his wealth is to teach his children the joy and fulfillment that can come from a life of helping those less fortunate. He decided that he would begin to teach his children (while they are young) about this connection to meaningful money and purposeful living by setting up donor-advised funds in each of the children's name. Each year the children have the joyous task of finding a cause that they really care about and making a gift to an approved charity. They not only are learning to give, but they also are learning to live with their eyes wide open to the needs of others and to the possibilities of making a difference.

By sharing his story with clients, Brooks is able to stir a dialogue around wealth and wealth building that touches on one of the chief fears of parents with money: how do I teach my kids the proper values around money? Advisors need not be afraid to offer creative approaches to answering some of the emotional issues tied to their clients' money.

## The Signature Statement of Wealth

We could use our money to buy the fanciest car in the world, but somebody has already done that. We could build a mansion that rises like a castle to the sky but there will always be a bigger, better, more amazing home than the one we build. People are looking to build something that hands and rust and decay cannot destroy. They seek an eternal container for their best selves, a vehicle for leaving their unique signature upon this planet. This container of dreams and inspiration is the result of the philanthropic pulse and charitable effort.

This generation of investors has decided that they don't need to be Bill Gates or Warren Buffett to make a difference in the world with their money. And, like Bill and Warren, they have decided that they don't have to be dead either. They want to be present to see the fruits of their charitable inclinations. The advisor who understands this and encourages the venture philanthropy conversation will see a whole new brand of charitable opportunity opening up.

We can do better than writing checks for tax purposes. We can invest our hearts, the sum of our experiences and our material gain, and leave a truly meaningful mark on this world—a signature that seals who we are and what matters most to us.

The last big, money-moving transition dialogue after retirement and preceding death most likely will be the investment of assets in matters of the heart, through charitable and purposeful giving. The advisor who connects with the heart can play a decisive role in helping clients change the world according to their personal vision for doing so.

## ReSOULution

Help clients to understand that the estate planning/legacy issues related to their money originate in the heart and soul, that ultimately the direction that they give to their money is a material animation of what stirs their pulse and gives their life meaning.

# Bibliography

AARP, "How America Can Grow Older and Prosper: Working in Retirement Is Increasingly an Expectation"; available at www.aarp.org/research/blueprint/overstatedproblem/working_in_retirement_is_increasingly_an_expectati.html.

AARP, "What Older Workers Want from Work," April 2004; Available at www.aarp.org/money/careers/employerresourcecenter/trends/a2004-04-20-olderworkers.html.

American Institute of Stress, "Job Stress"; available at www.stress.org/job.htm.

Bernstein, William. *The Birth of Plenty: How the Prosperity of the Modern World Was Created.* New York: McGraw-Hill, 2004.

Berry, Leonard L., and Neeli Bendapudi. "Clueing in Customers." *Harvard Business Review,* February 2003.

Commission on Public Trust and Private Enterprise, "Findings and Recommendations." (New York: The Conference Board, 2003); available at www.conference-board.org/knowledge/governCommission.cfm.

Consumer Federation of America, "Large Majority of Workers Risk Financial Exposure in Event of Disability, Survey Finds." Press release, April 23, 2001; available at www.consumerfed.org/pdfs/ltddisability.pdf.

De Soto, Hernando. *The Mystery of Capital: Why Capitalism Triumphs in the West and Fails Everywhere Else.* New York: Basic Books, 2003.

Derman, Emanuel. *My Life as a Quant: Reflections on Physics and Finance.* Hoboken, NJ: John Wiley & Sons, 2004.

Diliberto, Roy. *Financial Planning—the Next Step: A Practical Approach to Merging Your Clients' Money with Their Lives.* Denver, CO: FPA Press, 2006.

Disability Insurance Resource Center. "Disability Insurance Statistics." www.di-resource-center.com/statistics.html.

"Doing Well by Doing Good." *The Economist,* April 20, 2000; available at www.economist.com/business/displaystory.cfm?story_id=E1_PDQTTJ&CFID=26606313&CFTOKEN=65790723.

Easterlin, Richard A. "Explaining Happiness." *Proceedings of the National Academy of Sciences of the United States,* May 23, 2003; available at www.pnas.org/cgi/content/full/100/19/11176?maxtoshow=&HITS=10&hits=10&RESULTFORMAT=&fulltext=richard+easterlin&searchid=1&FIRSTINDEX=0&resourcetype=HWCIT.

Expedia.com. "2007 Vacation Deprivation Survey™" (conducted by Harris Interactive); available at http://media.expedia.com/media/content/expus/graphics/promos/vacations/Expedia_International_Vacation_Deprivation_Survey_Results_2007.pdf.

Fears, Darryl. "Boomers' Burdens: Their Kids, Parents." *Washington Post,* December 10, 2005; available at www.washingtonpost.com/wp-dyn/content/article/2005/12/09/AR2005120901643.html.

Frankl, Viktor E. *Man's Search for Meaning.* Boston, MA: Beacon Press, 2007.

Frankl, Viktor E. *The Doctor and the Soul: From Psychotherapy to Logotherapy.* New York: Vintage, 1986.

Galinsky, Ellen, James T. Bond, Stacy S. Kim, Lois Backon, Erin Brownfield, and Kelly Sakai. "Overworked in America: When the Way We Work Becomes Too Much." Families & Work Institute: 2005; www.familiesandwork.org/index.asp?PageAction=VIEWPROD&ProdID=136.

Good Morning America/ABC News Online. "Americans Embrace Ancient Practice of Yoga: Transforming an Ancient Exercise for Body and Mind to Make It Fit Modern Needs," March 26, 2005; available at http://abcnews.go.com/GMA/Health/story?id=615557&page=1.

Greenberg, Ilan. "Billy the Kid Grows Up." *The Industry Standard,* June 12, 2000; available at www.thestandard.com/article/0,1902,15543,00.html.

Greene, Brian. *The Fabric of the Cosmos.* New York: Penguin Science Press, 2005.

Herper, Matthew. "Now It's a Fact: Money Doesn't Buy Happiness." *Forbes.com,* September 23, 2004; available at http://moneycentral.msn.com/content/invest/forbes/P95294.asp.

Hill, Dan. *Emotionomics: Winning Hearts and Minds.* Edina, MN: Adams Business & Professional, 2007).

Hitti, Miranda. "Sleep Deprivation May Impair Memory: Staying Up All Night Makes for Fuzzy Memories, Study Shows." *WebMD Medical News,* February 12, 2007; available at www.webmd.com/sleep-disorders/news/20070213/sleep-deprivation-may-impair-memory.

Honorè, Carl. *In Praise of Slowness: How a Worldwide Movement is Challenging the Cult of Speed.* New York: HarperOne, 2005).

Individual Finance and Insurance Decisions Centre. www.ifid.ca/index.html.

Investor Relations. "Letters from the Founder." http://investor.google.com/ipo_letter.html.

Kahler, Rick, and Kathleen Fox. *Conscious Finance: Uncover Your Hidden Money Beliefs and Transform the Role of Money in Your Life* (Rapid City, SD: FoxCraft, Inc., 2005).

Kirchheimer, Sid. "Sleep Deprivation Leads to Trouble Fast: Losing Just 2 Hours of Nightly Sleep Hinders Thinking, Memory." *WebMD Medical News,* March 14, 2003; availableathttp://women.webmd.com/news/20030314/sleep-deprivation-leads-to-trouble-fast.

Mauboussin, Michael. *More Than You Know: Finding Financial Wisdom in Unconventional Places.* New York: Columbia University Press, 2007.

McGee, Susan. "Power Donors." *Barron's,* November 28, 2005; available at http://foundationcenter.org/pnd/news/story.jhtml?id=124000010.

Mental Heath America. "Americans Reveal Top Stressors, How They Cope." (Press Release, Alexandria, VA, November 16, 2006; available at www.mentalhealthamerica.net/index.cfm?objectid=ABD3DC4E-1372–4D20-C8274399C9476E26.

Mishel, Lawrence, Jared Bernstein, and Heather Boushey, *The State of Working in America 2002–2003*. Washington, DC: Economic Institute, 2003. Published by Cornell University Press; available at www.epi.org/content.cfm/books_swa2002_swa2002intro.

Meyerson, Bruce. "Many Baby Boomers Creating Personalized Family Foundations." *Arizona Daily Star,* April 5, 2004.

Pew Research Center. "Who's Feeling Rushed?" February 28, 2006; available at http://pewresearch.org/pubs/302/whos-feeling-rushed http://pewresearch .org/pubs/302/whos-feeling-rushed.

Quinn, Jacqueline. "The Metamorphosis of Retirement." *Journal of Financial Planning,* April 2001; available at www.fpanet.org/journal/articles/2001_Issues/jfp0401-art1.cfm.

Rajgopal, Shiva, Campbell Harvey, and John Gram, "Value Destruction and Financial Reporting Decisions." *Financial Analysts Journal* 62(6) (November/December 2006): 27–39.

"Report: Most Executives Work 50-Hour-Plus Weeks," *CIO,* April 28, 2006; available at www.cio.com/article/25090/Report_Most_Executives_Work_Hour_Plus_Weeks.

Royal Swedish Academy of Sciences. "The Sveriges Riksbank Prize in Economic Sciences in Memory of Alfred Nobel 2002"; from the press release available at http://nobelprize.org/nobel_prizes/economics/laureates/2002/press.html.

Russonello, Belden, and Stewart Research/Strategy/Management. "In the Middle: A Report on Multicultural Boomers Coping with Family and Aging Issues." AARP, July 2001; available at www.aarp.org/research/housing-mobility/caregiving/aresearch-import-789-D17446.html.

Samuelson, Judith. "A Critical Mass for the Long Term" featured in "Breakthrough Ideas for 2006." *Harvard Business Review,* February 2006.

Salmansohn, Karen, and Don Zinzell. *How to be Happy, Dammit: A Cynic's Guide to Spiritual Happiness*. Berkeley, CA: Celestial Arts, 2001.

Stein, Michael. *The Prosperous Retirement: Guide to the New Reality.* Boulder, CO: Emstco, LLC, 1998.

Weatherford, Jack. *The History of Money.* New York: Three Rivers Press, 1998).

Wolfbein, Seymour. *Work in American Society.* Glenview, IL: Scott, Foresman: 1971.

Zweig, Jason. *Your Money and Your Brain: How the New Science of Neuroeconomics Can Help Make You Rich.* New York: Simon & Schuster, 2007.

# Index